I0170676

Our deepest fear is not that we are inadequate. Our deepest fear is that we are powerful beyond measure.[1]

— MARIANNE WILLIAMSON

LIBRARY OF CONGRESS CONTROL NUMBER: 2018901352
Copyright © 2018 by Chandra Broadnax-Payne

TABLE OF CONTENTS

Acknowledgments

Everything I am and everything I will be I owe to my God for giving me life and the experiences—good and bad—that have helped to shape me into the woman I am today. A huge thank you to my wonderful supportive husband, Chris. I did it, honey! Special thanks to my bestie and sister-friend Paula for always believing in me no matter how far-fetched my ideas seemed. Thanks to my Mom, Harriet, for being the first person to introduce me to books. I watched her read an average of one to two books each weekend and thought it was the coolest thing. Hence my love for books. To my sister Chyna, thank you for always listening to my ideas even when you thought they were lame (as you say). To my niece Sage—I dedicate this book to you. I want you to know that any dream you have, no matter how big or small, is always possible. I love you munchkin. Now you can go back to daycare a true superstar!

Introduction

I was once told by a very good friend that my life story is like Joseph Campbell's interpretation of the Hero's Journey. In his interpretation, there are three acts. In the first act, the hero is called to adventure but is reluctant. In the second act, the hero faces adversity but ultimately overcomes it. In the final act, the hero defeats their enemy and returns home transformed. The hero then uses the knowledge and wisdom gained in battle to help his or her fellow humans.

When my friend first mentioned it, I had no idea who Joseph Campbell was or what this Hero's Journey business was all about. When I read his synopsis of the journey, I couldn't believe my eyes. It did indeed describe the path my life had taken. Most works about the Hero's Journey show the hero as a male figure, but as I read the synopsis I saw myself in the story.

To give you to a better of understanding of my story, let me take you back to the beginning. I was born to a single mother in the projects of Brooklyn, NY, in the `70s. I was like every other child in my neighborhood, poor and trying to figure out life. Growing up, I witnessed prostitution, drugs, and crime on a regular basis. I had no hope back then. I often felt miserable and awkward. I was also taller than most of my classmates, and only boy's clothing fit me. I was called Olive Oyl on many occasions. Kids can be cruel.

My life changed when I met Mrs. Giovanni, my middle school teacher, at PS 273. I will never forget the valuable gift she gave me: possibilities. Every day for at least an hour, she would turn classical music on for the students during recess. We would listen to the likes of Beethoven, Mozart, and Bach— just to name a few. She would encourage us to use the time to relax, but instead, I used the time to daydream about my future. I stopped focusing on my neighborhood and environment and began focusing on my dreams.

You can either focus on your dreams and your future or you can focus on what's in front of you right now. You make the choice!

I enjoyed this quiet time so much I started daydreaming outside of the classroom. I would go home and play music and write short stories and poems. I even published a poem in my twenties that I had written when I was fourteen. I wrote stories to escape my environment. I did this for many years, knowing that my situation wasn't permanent. One day, I wouldn't have to worry about whether or not we would have enough food to eat or have enough school clothes. I knew, deep down, that there was something greater out there for me.

Fast forward to adulthood. My greatness was put on hold. I maneuvered through the challenges of establishing a career, struggling with a lack of purpose, and getting through difficult relationships. A nice vehicle, a fancy apartment, and a modest-paying corporate job masked my sadness. I'd thought all those things would bring me joy, but eventually began to realize they didn't. Despite my outward success, I still felt a yearning for something more. It was during this time that I began to walk down a dark path of drinking a little too frequently, often alone. I no longer enjoyed my job and was working with people I did not like. I was afraid to stand up for myself and secretly operated in a mode of low self-esteem. All the negative feelings slowly began to manifest into depression.

In my darkest hour, I contemplated suicide as I sat sobbing on my bedroom floor. In that crucial moment I made the decision to attend therapy and find a church. Thank goodness for good therapists and God. Several years later, I still find myself struggling sometimes, but I am a much happier person now, living my purpose and no longer hanging out with my old buddy, low self-esteem. She can kick rocks!

I'm assuming if you're reading this book that there are some areas of your life that you would like to shed so you can step into your greatness. Maybe you drink too much or suffer from depression. Maybe you did all the right things—went to college, met the man of your dreams, had 2.5 children, and landed your dream job—but you feel like you're living a lukewarm life. Or maybe you're financially comfortable and want for nothing, but still feel unfulfilled for some reason or another.

You are not alone, and I am so very proud of you, my sister, for making a commitment to yourself. From the very first moment you opened up this book, you made an important decision to reclaim your life and step into your greatness.

Congratulations! Take a moment to give yourself kudos for recognizing that you could be living a more fulfilled life. This book is the first step toward helping you realize that dream. I hope it will serve as an eye-opener for anyone wondering why they feel stuck or how to show up and stop playing small in this world. It *will* require you to do some work, often in the form of self-reflection. You'll need to be honest. But you can do it! I'm rooting for you; we're all rooting for you to stand strong in who you were created to be. And I can't wait to see you when you've realized your greatness.

PS: There are several mentions of God throughout the book, as he is the head of my life. However, I am a Christian who believes that everyone should have the right to practice or not practice a religion of their choice. God may mean something different to you, and that's just fine.

PART I

TAP INTO YOUR CREATOR

Take a Backseat

Just relax and let GOD be GOD. [2]

— Joyce Meyer

I have lots of personal experience trying to drive the car called life. For years I did what I wanted, when I wanted, and how I wanted. It worked out pretty good for a while—until I crashed. I remember the crash vividly. It culminated in me sitting on my bedroom floor one day, in tears, asking God to end my life and trying to think of the least painful method to commit suicide.

To those looking at my life from the outside, I lived the picture-perfect life. I had a nice career, a loving relationship, and a good education. Throughout my career, I'd served as a mentor and did lots of volunteer work in my community, including serving on the board for a well-known non-profit organization for women. Yet, despite my success, deep down I was secretly a hot mess, a disaster waiting to happen.

You see, no career or MBA could save me from myself. I didn't realize it at the time, but I was suffering from depression. It would take a therapist diagnosis for me to understand what was happening to me. I can unashamedly say that therapy helped to save my life. I learned about myself through therapy. I experienced many revelations and eye-opening moments. My wish for you, after reading this book, is that you are able to have a revelation or two as well.

I want to share how it all began because I believe that I was depressed years before my diagnosis. I now believe it started when I was a child and continued, off and on, for many years after.

In 1976, I was born in Brookdale Hospital to a loving, quiet mother and a loud, rambunctious father. My dad faded in and out of the picture over the years, leaving my mom to be a single mother of two young girls. Though she was often quiet and kept to herself, she did the best job raising us she could. But with one check feeding three mouths, we did not have very much in the way of finances and we had to take up residence in the projects of East New York. If any of you are familiar with East NY in the late '70s, you know it was the peak of the crack and heroin epidemic.

Thank God my sister and I never chose that path; it wouldn't have been hard. We lived on the top floor of our building. For some reason, all the addicts and dope dealers thought the top floor provided some sort of privacy, so that's where they all took up residence. Which meant every time we stepped outside the apartment, we had to step over some addict who was either on a high or coming down from a high, then walk past the dope dealers supplying the addicts.

If that wasn't enough to scare the heebie-jeebies out of a young child, we attended school during a time when jumping or slashing people was the "in thing" to do. Not only did I fear the dealers and the addicts, but I also had to worry about getting jumped or having my face slashed.

Looking back, I probably started to become depressed as a preteen. I stood several feet taller than most of my classmates, which made me feel awkward. On top of that, I was shy and often felt different. My mom did the best she could, but there were plenty of times that I felt stressed because we couldn't afford clothes and sometimes even food. As a result,

I became angry and withdrawn.

I know some of you might think "Well, there are lots of people that grow up poor, and they don't become depressed." Well, hooray for them. I wish I could say that was my story—but it wasn't. And unless you have experienced growing up in the projects, or fearing for your life, or having a grown man lock you in a taxi and tell you what he wanted to do to you as a preteen, or having a babysitter you trusted touch you inappropriately one day—you will never understand the impact that kind of environment can have on a child. To say the least, it was traumatizing. These events had a devastating impact on me. As a result, I became even more introverted than I already was. Because we were poor, I didn't feel like I was worth much. And when you're poor, people treat you like you're poor—so you never forget it. To tell you the truth, I felt invisible. I held on to this feeling of being invisible all the way to college.

I grew up in a family in which going to college was a distant dream, and you were lucky if you finished high school. Yet, I knew I wanted to do something different; something more. Plus, my father made it very clear that he wanted me to attend college, and I always did what my parents told me; that's how I was raised. As a result, I was the first person on my mother's side of the family to graduate from college.

Boy, did I have some good times in college. Some I won't mention in this book; you can use your imagination. But I did what most kids that age did; I partied, made bad decisions, and drank. The problem was—I couldn't stop drinking after the partying was over. I began to drink alone at one point. But thank goodness for an observant mother: she noticed and nipped that in the bud. Although my mother only stands at five feet and three and a half inches tall, she is one of the strongest women I know. She's never been one to yell or curse to get her point across, but when she speaks, you listen. She demands respect. I remember the summer she caught wind of my drinking like it was yesterday. She confronted me and made it clear I was to stop immediately. She said, "You better not be drinking. If I ever catch you drinking . . . ." And that was that. She didn't have to say any more. I respected my mom, so I stopped.

After graduating, I landed a job with a major financial institution and got my first apartment. Life was pretty good for a while. I was in charge of steering my life in the direction I wanted to go. I drove my life, only getting minor traffic infractions, nothing I couldn't recover from. The important thing was that I was in control of the car. If you're a control freak, you know exactly what I'm talking about. That satisfactory experience you get from being in charge. As long as I was in control, I was happy. But the moment things didn't go my way, my world would crumble. I now realize that during most of my life, I haven't felt in control. I was at the mercy of others, and they failed me time and time again. Because of that, as an adult, I was very conscious of the fact that I felt my best when I was in control.

I would date people I knew I didn't have a future with; usually men who were either dating someone else or dating an alcohol bottle. That way, I didn't have to worry about commitments and feelings. I did what I wanted and didn't have to answer to any man because we were technically not in a relationship. In the beginning, controlling my relationships, or lack thereof, felt good. In the end, that control left me feeling empty. None of it made me feel good in the long run. Dating these men with no commitment just helped me to pass the time. Deep down, I knew it didn't feel right.

Despite this, I kept driving and driving. Through every situation and every relationship over the years, God would provide subtle and gentle nudges telling me to pull over and let him drive. Put down the bottle, you're drinking a little too much. That person is not your friend. Don't waste your time with this man. At the time, it sounded like noise. I refused to listen. I wanted to do things my way, so I continued to drive. I knew I needed to find a church, but I didn't. My uncle was a pretty well-known pastor in NY, and as a child I was forced to attend his church every week. When I got old enough to make my own decisions, I stopped going to church. I continued to drive.

This rebellion went on for several years, ending only when I lost control and crashed. Can I share a secret with you? In hindsight, that crash was the best thing that ever happened to me. You may think I've lost my marbles, but I have never been so serious when I say it was the absolute best thing that could have happened to me. Sitting on my bedroom floor contemplating suicide saved my life. Although it was a near fatal crash, it allowed me to get rid of some bad habits and people that didn't have my best interests at heart. It was part of my renewal process, and I came back stronger, more relentless, and more fearless. As painful as the crash was, it taught me so many lessons, one of which is that God wants the best for me, and that my best can't compare to his best on any level. Only He knows what that best is for me, even when I *think* I know best. I had to acknowledge that I can't see what lies ahead on this road called life. I learned to sit in the backseat and trust that God's destination would be the best one for me.

Reflection:

Grab a sheet of paper or a journal and take a few minutes to really conduct an honest assessment of your life. Write down the answers to these questions:

- Do you struggle with the need to be in control?

- What do you feel the need to control?

- Where do you think this tendency came from? Your childhood, your parents, simply being let down by people, or something else?

- Are there any areas of your life that you could stand to take a backseat on and let your God/the Universe steer?

- How could your life improve if you let your God/the Universe take over?

Slowly begin your climb toward the backseat and let God have the steering wheel. I promise you the destination will be better than you can imagine.

TIP: Carry a journal or notebook with you at all times, as this will be an important step in capturing your feelings, and emotions on this journey.

Guard Your Thoughts

You are today where your thoughts have brought you;
you will be tomorrow where your thoughts take you.[3]

— James Allen

Once upon a time I subscribed to the narrative that I have nothing unique to offer. I would ask myself, "Why do I feel like I'm special?" I can't write a book. I can't run a business. What could I offer people? I'm just a poor kid from the projects. Most people from the projects never make it out. Why would I be any different? My beloveds, I can honestly say now—I was a victim of my own thoughts.

But honey, let me tell you—I am proud to say I am no longer a victim. I got tired of playing that card. It got old. And now, I am a heck of a lot more optimistic. This was one of my favorite chapters to write because looking back, I can see how much I've grown, and I know that I grew so much because I changed the way I think.

I didn't realize that my life was the way it was because of my thought process. I know now that I did not deserve to be touched inappropriately by anyone, and I did not wish that into existence. However, my beliefs about being "less than" because of what happened to me and where I grew up made me feel inferior. As a result, I made inferior decisions. In essence, my thoughts set me up for failure. Even though, deep down, I wanted to do better, my thoughts kept me pigeonholed to an inferior way of thinking. This showed when I would refer to myself as stupid. It showed when I would date someone who had abusive tendencies and would stay because I kept telling myself that no one else would want me. Oh, but thank goodness for growth! I did not know then what I know now: that death and life lie in the power of the tongue. When you really think about it, where do your words come from? They come from your thoughts. That is why we must be extra careful about managing our thoughts.

Watch your thoughts; they become words. Watch your words; they become actions. Watch your actions, they become habits. Watch your habits, they become character. Watch your character; it becomes your destiny. [4]

— *Frank Outlaw*

If we take that line of thought one step further, death and life lie first in the power of your thoughts, since you have to first formulate a thought in your mind before you speak it. I am lazy, I am unworthy, I'll never get out of debt, and I'm not marriage material. All of these are negative thoughts that many of us say to ourselves on a daily basis. Imagine how harmful these words can be when you say them over and over to yourself.

Words, my friends, have the power to shift the direction of your life. Isn't that scary and amazing at the same time? Think about it. If you refer to yourself as stupid, unworthy, or broke, guess what will manifest in your life? All those things you have said about your life. What's amazing is that we manifest what we think. Our thoughts and words have the power to create our reality. That's a crazy amount of power that we have. So why not use our powers to produce something meaningful in our lives?

My sister, if you have the power to shift the trajectory of your life, why not shift it for the better? Begin to use phrases like "I am worthy," "I am strong," "I am debt free," "I am the CEO and not the employee," and watch the power of manifestation in your life. You will be surprised at what the universe brings you.

Reflection:

Take out a piece of paper or your journal and write down your answers to the following questions:

- Have you (in the past or currently) had any negative thoughts about your life?

- What were they?

- What are some of the negative words you say to yourself?

- What are some of the negative words you say about yourself in conversation with others?

- Can you think of examples where these negative words served to create your reality?

- Can you think of examples where you have used positive words to create your reality?

Write down the negative words you say to yourself, and then write positive words beside them. Replace those negative words with the positive ones in your mind. Now, make a conscious effort to only use the new positive words. You'll be amazed at how much words—even those words you never say out loud—shape your mood, perspective, and life.

Embrace Your Gifts

Don't ask yourself what the world needs. Ask yourself what makes you come alive and then go and do that. Because what the world needs is people who have come alive.[5]

— Howard Washington Thurman

I've always felt different. I grew up writing short stories and poetry. I was an intense and deep thinker. While most teens my age were interested in hanging out, I was interested in spending time alone, with my thoughts. Don't get me wrong—I had my share of partying. I would go to a teen club several times a month during my last few years of high school. It was a safe environment for teens. I was always mature for my age, so my mom let me go. I'd go and have a blast with my friends, but at the end of the day I would always come home to my thoughts.

My thoughts revolved around some pretty serious topics. I used to wonder why I was placed here on this earth, why I felt different. I'd wonder how I could be a normal teenager and still embrace who I was at my core. Some of my stories and poems dealt with controversial topics, such as racism, sexism, romantic relationships, and difficult family dynamics. Pretty weird for a young teen, right? Well, if you're thinking I was odd, just know you weren't the only one. When I told people what I was writing or thinking about, they would look at me strangely. Because of this, I became hesitant to share that side of me. However, I continued to write, and I am so glad I did. Those deep thoughts and self-reflections allowed me to use my gifts. Years later, my creativity continues to flow. If I had listened to those that ridiculed me, there is a real chance that I may never have written this book. All that creativity that I nourished year after year after year has allowed me to embrace my gifts. Now, when people ask me what I do, I proudly answer: I'm an author.

It wasn't always easy to embrace who I was. Although my father wasn't around all the time, when he did come around he always had little nuggets of wisdom that he would leave me with. I credit my father for helping me with that. It was one of the best lessons from my dad. I can recall a few conversations where I expressed to him how different I felt because I knew I was weird. He'd reply, "Mommy [yes, that is my father's nickname for me], don't ever refer to yourself that way." He would insist that I wasn't weird. That instead, I was special in a unique and beautiful way. That my differences were great things, not bad things. One of the things I love about my father is his ability to make me believe in my gifts and talents. In the beginning, his words would go in one ear and out the other. It would take many years before I understood what he was trying to impart to me, but I finally got it.

One day, I woke up, and it was like a lightbulb had gone off. I'd finally learned to embrace what makes me who I am—and girlfriend, I am loving it! I no longer think I'm strange, weird, or awkward. After reading this book, *you* might think I'm strange, weird, or awkward—and that's okay! You have a right to your opinion, and I've realized that the most important thing is I no longer think those negative things about myself. Instead, I use words like magnificent, amazing, and absolutely beautiful to describe myself. And that doesn't even include my physical body—yet. Like everyone else, I am a work in progress. My goal is to create a healthier body that matches what's on the inside of me. In addition to this, I am no longer embarrassed by my abilities. I'm a creative artist who embraces who she is. My book and future products depend on my ability to embrace who I am and all my gifts.

Maybe you don't sit in your room for hours writing stories or curled up on the floor with a blanket and a novel. Your gift may involve your ability to be extremely organized. It can be anything. For example, I have a friend who is a master organizer. I have never seen anyone plan the way she does. I'll admit, every now and then I like to joke with her about how organized she is, but anytime I need help organizing my thoughts or a room in my house, she is the first person I call because I know that organization is a gift she has and operates in comfortably.

Have you ever stopped to think about your gifts? Are you really good with numbers? Maybe accounting is your thing. Do you enjoy helping others achieve success and navigate through life? Maybe you would make an ideal life coach. Are you really good at debating ideas and thoughts? Maybe there's a courtroom waiting for you.

Whatever your gift, I encourage you to embrace it. Can you imagine how awesome this world would be if each and every person were operating in their gift? No matter what your gift is, spend time nurturing it. Love up on it and give it room to breathe so that it can flourish. Your thoughts about your gift are the soil that will either help your gift flourish and develop into a beautiful flower or will poison the seedling and help it die. You choose.

Reflection:

Take out a piece of paper or your journal and write down your answers to the following questions:

- What are your gifts?

- Do you fully embrace them?

- If not, what gifts do you have that you haven't fully embraced yet?

- Are there certain things that others have told you that you do really well?

- Who could you serve with your gifts if you began to use them?

- Who are you doing a disservice if you don't use your gifts?

Now, make a commitment to embrace and operate in your gifts—starting today. You may feel awkward, but keep at it. Eventually, you'll believe in your gifts and will get comfortable operating within your gifts. It just takes you starting, one day at a time.

Pray

Relying on God has to begin all over again every day as if nothing had yet been done.[6]

— C.S. Lewis

As I sat down to write this chapter, I asked God for a title and heard the word, "Pray." It came to me very clearly and distinctly—pray. I'll admit, at the time I had no idea what prayer had to do with loving yourself. That is the basic underlying premise of this book: to learn to love yourself. But as I continued to ask the Lord to reveal his desire for this chapter to me, my pen began to move feverishly across the page. I suddenly saw all the enemies that we have to fight every day to be able to love ourselves more.

We were all created by a higher power, by God or the Universe or Spirit. Whatever your religion or spirituality, that power did not create you to hate the person you see in the mirror. I understand how difficult it can be to see the beauty in yourself at times. That is why you must stay in connection to your source, your higher power. And the best way to stay connected is through prayer. Prayer is the lifeline to your source that is always open twenty-four hours a day, seven days a week.

If you turn on a TV anywhere in America, you are met with gorgeous actresses and entertainers. These women ooze beauty and sex. Take Beyoncé, for example. Everyone knows who she is, and if you don't, you should probably come out of the hole you're living in. Beyoncé could walk into the grocery store in pajamas with a cup of coffee in hand and we would all stare and wonder where to buy that pajama set. I'm a huge fan of Bey, but my point is—we are too fixated with what we see on TV and in magazines. So many women rely on these images as a benchmark for beauty. This is unhealthy and unrealistic thinking as a lot of the images have been photoshopped. Despite this, if we don't meet the standards we see, then we believe we aren't beautiful. This is one of societies lies. We are taught that to be beautiful, you can't be above a size six. That you have to have a gap in between your thighs to show how thin you are. That you can't have any crow lines under your eyes. That you must inject collagen in your lips so they can be fuller. If that isn't bad enough, we've subscribed to the notion that we must inject our butts to look larger. Who came up with that idea? Why not just wear clothes that are flattering to your unique body shape? At the end of the day, the surgeries you have take away from your natural God-given beauty. Stop spending thousands of dollars to change your body. Stop emulating the stars and entertainers. When you idolize them, you lose sight of yourself and begin to see fault in your own natural beauty.

Did you know the United States' cosmetic industry is worth $54.89 billion dollars?[6] Who has that kind of money to spend? We do! We spend the money, feeling like we need to because we want to look like the beautiful print models and television stars. We are lured by anything that sparkles in front of us, and that will cause our own sparkle to die out if we are not careful. This is disheartening but true. How do we change this type of thinking, you ask? Through prayer.

Every person has to contend with society's opinion of them on a daily basis. Trust me—it is easy to let society's opinion govern your life. It happens all the time. It happens in the workplace when you look around the meeting and not one woman in the room has a hair out of place or is above a certain dress size. Maybe they all even sound the same. It happens every time you tell your child she doesn't need the ice cream and that a salad would help her lose five pounds. Now do you understand the importance of prayer? It is so easy to get caught up in people's opinion of us. This world cares about material and superficial things. Meanwhile, God cares about our hearts and what is inside of us. That is why it is so important to pray and read *your* scripture. It is only through prayer (time with *your* God) and scripture (the word of *your* God) that we will discover how abundant God's love for us truly is. Scripture reminds us that we were created in his image and that our value lies in much more than material items. Prayer provides the sustenance that we need in order to stay strong in mind.

It is impossible to understand how magnificent you were created to be if you don't have a connection to your creator. You deserve to walk in your power and in your beauty. You were uniquely designed and it is time you accepted that. I encourage you to pray and strengthen your connection to your creator so he can help you strengthen your beliefs about yourself. It is my deep connection and prayer to my source, God, that helps me shift my beliefs about myself. I pray he will do the same for you.

Reflection:

Are you struggling with your prayer life? If so, seek to draw closer to God. Here are some ways to do that:

- Find a quiet spot in your home dedicated to spending time with the Lord. Don't make it a chore; make it a fun time catching up with an old friend who loves you. God will reveal his love for you, and that will strengthen the love you have for yourself.

- Sit outside in nature, take a walk in the park, or visit a lake or body of water. This will help clear your mind from distractions.

- Meditate every day. This will also help clear your mind from distractions so that you can hear from God.

Do you notice a pattern here? It really doesn't matter whether you're in a room in your home or outside in nature. God is wherever you are because he lives within you. The point is to spend time in stillness and he will reveal himself to you. Plus, prayer is free. Wouldn't you rather spend no money and gain the best advice ever? It takes little to no time. Start your prayer life today.

PART II

LIVE UNAPOLOGETICALLY

Honor Yourself

Self-care is never a selfish act—it is simply good stewardship of the only gift I have, the gift I was put on earth to offer to others.[8]

— **Parker Palmer**

How many times have you heard the saying "you only live once"? If I had a dollar for every time I heard someone say that, I'd be rich. The term has been around since 2004, when TV personality Adam Mesh first said it. Most recently, it was made popular when a well-known rap artist by the name of Drake affectionately used it in his rap song, "YOLO (You Only Live Once)."[9] Simply put, it means: you only live once, so why not live it up. I agree one hundred percent that we only live once. However, I want to take it further; if we only live once, then why not make it our best life? Living your best life doesn't mean going out to party every night, getting drunk or high. It doesn't mean spending every dollar you make or sleeping with everyone that says hi to you. That is not and will never be, in my opinion, a way to live your best life. To me, making the best out of your life means honoring who you are.

My friends, we are only given one body, so why not honor it? When you honor yourself, you are making a commitment to take care of yourself. This means honoring everything that is a part of you: your mind, body, *and* soul. There are several ways to do this, which we will discuss in this chapter. Let's cover the physical act of honoring your body first, as that is probably the easiest to understand.

The act of honoring your body can involve things like exercise, meditation, and practicing healthy eating habits—just to name a few. It also means steering clear of any type of mind-altering substances, like drugs and alcohol. Now, there is nothing wrong with alcohol in moderation. The problem comes when people drink in excess. I know you're probably thinking that taking care of yourself is easy; it's not like it's rocket science. And you're absolutely right; it's not rocket science. But if it were so easy, then why don't more people take care of their bodies? How many of you have a family member that is always complaining about being tired, or always telling you about their various aches and pains? I've been that family member. It wasn't until I started doing Pilates and gentle yoga that I stopped feeling sluggish every day.

My point is, we spend too much time complaining about aches and pains, about the extra twenty pounds we put on, or about the fact that none of our clothes fit anymore. The list of complaints goes on and on. Yet we do nothing to change. We are so comfortable with the habit of complaining that we neglect to form a habit of doing. For those of you that already make exercise a part of your routine, I applaud you.

According to a 2016 article on Mayo Clinic, the benefits to exercise include: controlling weight, combatting health conditions and disease, improving mood, boosting energy, promoting better sleep, and putting the spark back into your sex life. And lastly—it can be fun.[10] With benefits like that, why is it so hard to do? I'll tell you why. It's because we are quick to honor others but less than enthusiastic when it comes to honoring ourselves. If we truly honored ourselves and this one body we've been given, then it wouldn't be so hard to take care of it. Which is very disappointing.

How do we go from a habit of complaining to a habit of doing? This is the moment I know you've been waiting for. I can see you sitting on the edge of your seat, waiting for the secret to overcoming the exercise rut or eating unhealthily. Here it goes . . . it all starts in your mind. That's right. It all starts in your mind. You must first find your *why*. In college, I was a very thin 115 pounds. I didn't need to exercise to lose weight, but I loved exercising because it helped me to release energy, and it was fun. I even became a certified aerobics instructor. By the time I reached my mid-thirties, it was less exciting and more of a chore. I exercised sporadically to help keep my weight down when things started to widen in the lower half of my body. By the time I turned forty, I hated exercising. I had to constantly push myself. I would get started with a really good routine and within two to three weeks, my routine devolved into sitting on the couch telling myself how badly I needed to exercise while stuffing a piece of cake in my mouth. It got to the point where I was constantly sluggish, not sleeping well, and picking up weight. I got sick and tired of being sick and tired all the time—literally. My body was prone to viral infections and other illnesses because I wasn't taking care of it. I was too fatigued to exercise, which caused even more fatigue and exhaustion. I was also eating more fast foods at the time. If that wasn't enough, I also experienced a debilitating injury that left me unable to move my neck for almost a year.

Then, one day, the lightbulb went off and I remembered how much energy I used to have when I made exercise a part of my daily routine. So I began the journey of waking up at 5:15 a.m. to get some exercise in before starting my day. I'm not going to tell you that I don't hit the snooze button or wish that I could just lie in bed for another hour. There are plenty of times when I do. But getting up to exercise has become routine to the point where I've learned to stop thinking about the fact that it's 5:15 am; I just get out of bed without thinking about it. This practice has not only helped me to lose weight, but also to develop better sleep patterns. I've also learned a few recipes so I can eat out less and eat in more.

Maybe you're not a 5:15 a.m. kind of gal. Maybe you become super energized around noon. If that's the case, walk around your building for thirty minutes on your break. Or if your company has a gym, walk the treadmill for thirty minutes. Each person's body has different needs. Find out what your body needs and do it. The other thing you must do is watch what you eat. Being mindful of the foods you put into your body is as important as exercise. Are you eating fried foods, fattening foods, or lots of junk foods? If you are, then know you are setting your body up for failure.

I will be the first to admit that it isn't easy to develop a routine, but you have to remember your *why*. There were plenty days I wanted to give up, but I would remember how sluggish I felt when I didn't have an exercise routine. I thought about all my goals and dreams. All the things I wanted to accomplish. Then I asked my body, "Can you get me where I need to go?" If the honest answer was no, I got busy. There is no way I could be the great author and speaker I desire to be if I'm unable to lift myself out of bed every morning, and that's how bad things got after my injury. I could no longer enjoy the simple things in life, like picking up my niece after my sister gave birth to her, because I was ordered not to lift anything heavier than one pound. The other motivating factor was realizing how important I was to God, and acknowledging that if God thinks I'm so important, then I've got to honor the body he's given me.

What is your why? Do you want to be around for a long time to watch your kids grow and possibly have kids of their own? To help other people, or to stay on this journey with your partner or spouse for as long as you can? Whatever your why is, know that you can have all the things you desire, but you *have* to take care of yourself in order to have them. You can't expect to be around for grandchildren if you're smoking two packs of cigarettes a day, shooting drugs into your arm, or having unprotected sex with Tom, Dick, and Jane. Eventually, all those bad habits will catch up with you. Taking care of the one body you've been given will allow you to live a long, hopefully illness-free life. By living healthily, you could have fifty-plus years of marriage with your partner. You may even get to witness your grandchildren grow up to have children of their own. The list of benefits goes on and on.

Now that I have explained the benefits and ways to honor your physical body, let's delve into the second topic, which involves taking care of your emotional health.

Please note that the body and mind are equally important. For the purpose of driving home this point, I'd like to use the analogy of a car. Imagine your physical body as a car engine. Your emotional health is the motor oil that keeps your engine going. What happens if you don't keep up with the oil maintenance in your vehicle? It causes all kinds of damage to your engine. The same thing will happen to you if you don't conduct regular maintenance on your mind and emotional well-being. You will shut down, unable to function properly. That is why taking care of your emotional health is just as important as taking care of your physical body.

It saddens me to see people in the gym bench-pressing huge weights, doing exercises to make their bodies look like Dwayne "the Rock" Johnson, but neglecting to take care of their emotional health. Don't get me wrong; I cannot say enough good things about the Rock's body. But so often, on the outside their bodies are like a Greek God's, and on the inside—emotionally— they are fragile and on the verge of collapse. Don't let that be you. Take care of every single part of you. I say this because you deserve it. You deserve to be in the best emotional and physical state that you can be in.

What are some of the benefits of a healthy emotional state? You will experience increased joy. You'll have a healthier picture of yourself and healthier relationships. You'll be able to make better decisions because your mind will be clearer. Doesn't this sound exciting?

There are certain activities that will help you maintain your emotional health and well-being. Meditation and yoga to relieve stress are some of the most popular methods. Another tip is to stay away from unhealthy relationships and people. Practice mindfulness. Mindfulness helps you to stay focused on the present moment and not become overwhelmed and worried about the future. As a result, being mindful can reduce anxiety and stress and improve your mood.

And lastly, cultivate a spiritual practice. It is important to have a spiritual practice with whatever your higher power or source is. The spiritual practice will serve as the DNA to your soul. For me it is God. For you it may be God, Buddha, the Universe, or the Spirit. Whoever or whatever your source is, I encourage you to spend time with it. Your relationship with your source will allow you to operate at a higher emotional frequency and will help you make better decisions. For example, connecting to your source is important in times of stress because you will rely on that source instead of people during difficult times.

Your soul is the control tower to your mind and body. Your connection to it is critical, since the health of your mind and physical body depend on a healthy and strong soul. A control tower is useless if there is no power. That is why you must spend time every day ensuring that there is power in your control tower. Your mind, body, and life depend on it and will thank you for it.

Reflection:

Take out a piece of paper or your journal and write
down your answers to the following questions:

- What are some ways you can honor your body?

- Are there any barriers that prevent you from honoring your
  body? If so, think outside the box. How can you overcome
  those challenges? In my case, after my neck injury, I could no
  longer lift weights, do Zumba, or take step classes. Instead, I
  turned to yoga and Pilates, which are much easier on my body.

- What are some ways you can honor your emotional health?

- Are there any barriers that prevent you from
  honoring your emotional health?

- Take inventory of your spiritual practice. Are
  you happy with it? Is it feeding your soul?

- If not, what are some ways to strengthen your spiritual practice?

If you feel as though any area of your life is out of control, there
is nothing wrong with asking for help, either from a friend or
a professional. Anyone who tells you something is wrong with
asking for help should probably go seek help themselves.

Practice mindfulness to improve happiness and sleep, reduce stress, and
boost concentration. Included below are some mindfulness techniques:

- Practice meditation. Sit in silence in a comfortable
  position and focus on each breath.

- Practice stillness. Sit in silence for increasing amounts of time.

- Practice mindful eating. Eat when your body tells you
  to eat and stop when your body tells you it's full.

- Practice gratitude. Start by making a list of
  all the things you are grateful for.

Now begin honoring yourself.

Learn to Say No—And Mean It!

Let today mark a new beginning for you. Give yourself permission to say NO without feeling guilty, mean, or selfish. Anybody who gets upset and/or expects you to say YES all of the time clearly doesn't have your best interest at heart. Always remember: You have a right to say NO without having to explain yourself. Be at peace with your decisions. [11]

— Stephanie Lahart

Chances are you probably said no more as a child than as an adult. If you don't believe me, just go somewhere where children are present, like a store or the park, and listen carefully. You will hear an overabundance of the use of the word no.

I've watched countless children in stores tell their parents no. Child #1: "Jess, put that candy down, it's not yours," to which Jess would reply loudly, "No." Child #2: "Keisha, come back here so I can see you," to which Keisha replies "No." You get the point. Though young children haven't learned many words, they often master the word no early on. That is their go-to word; often their favorite word, besides momma.

Although I do not have children, I have a niece who is less than two years old and who has mastered the word already. When she was an infant, I would tell her I loved her, which made her smile. Now when I tell her I love her, she tells me "No"—to which I reply, "I still love you anyway, little girl."

I don't know about you, but I find children interesting, amazing, and inspirational. One thing I love about them is how strong and relentless they are. They are not afraid to stand up for what they believe in, even if it means pouring milk out of the sippy cup onto your recently mopped floor, or riding their bikes straight down a muddy hill only to stand up with a face full of mud and a big smile at the bottom. Children are fearless. I love to observe them because I believe we can learn many lessons from them. One of which is that it's fine to say no.

About two years ago, I watched a documentary in which criminals were interviewed about how they were able to commit crimes. One murderer implied that people make it easy to take advantage of them. I don't recall the specific example he used or the name of the film, but he basically implied that some people fall prey to others because they are afraid of hurting others' feelings. Let me break it down for you. If a criminal knocks on the door of an unsuspecting victim's house and asks to use the phone, the potential victim may oblige the criminal simply because he or she is afraid to hurt the criminal's feelings. Even though their gut tells them to be afraid, the potential victim will say yes because they feel uncomfortable saying no. This same psychopath also told the story of how he would offer to help women with their groceries. He talked about how he could see the quick flash of hesitation in their eyes, but they would agree anyway. That was how he would find his victims.

These examples are extreme but true. My beloveds, I'm not telling you to be paranoid and fearful. What I am saying is that if something doesn't feel right or doesn't sit well with you, then say no. I pray that you will never be in a situation with a psychopathic murderer, but you may be faced with other situations. Imagine that you're leaving a party and everyone has had something to drink. You don't want to get in your friend's car, but you do because you're afraid to say no. Or maybe the man you're dating is a serial cheater. You've broken up with him several times, yet he always manages to weasel his way back in your life because you are afraid to say no to him. What I want you to understand is that when you say no to others, it allows you to say yes to yourself.

There was a time when I would stay up at night wrestling with the thought of having to turn someone down. Even if I was right and it was in my best interest, it was still difficult. I eventually realized I didn't place value on my own needs and put the needs of others before my own. It may have hurt their feelings when I told them no, but I didn't see until years later how much it hurt me by *not* saying no. By saying yes to others all those times when I really wanted to say no, I was really saying no to me. When I got tired of all the sleepless nights and stressing myself out, I learned to say no. And Let me tell you, honey—I've never felt so liberated in my life.

Reflection:

Take out a piece of paper or your journal. List five areas of your life where you need to say no. Then, think about the questions below. Write out your answers underneath your list.

- How will saying no change some of your relationships? If saying no impacts your relationship negatively, meaning if someone becomes angry with you for saying no, then realize that this is not the friend or partner for you.

- Are there times at work when saying no would be beneficial?

- Are there times when you need to say no in your personal relationships?

- How would saying no make you feel better?

Use your voice. Speak up for yourself and say no to others so that you can say yes to yourself.

Become Your Own Champion

Champions keep playing until they get it right.[12]

— Billie Jean King

Take a moment to think about some of your heroes and what they have in common. I bet you could write a whole list of things you admire about them. Some of my heroes (or should I say "sheroes"?) are Oprah Winfrey, Serena Williams, and J.K. Rowling—just to name a few. Each of these women blazed trails that no one had dared before their time.

Take a moment and reflect on your own heroes or sheroes. Think about how excited you get when there is an article about one of them, or when they received a prestigious award for their work. While it is wonderful to read about your heroes or sheroes, have you ever stopped to think about the sacrifices they made to get to where they are? The number of doors that were closed in their faces before they became the people they are today? Tyler Perry, for example, didn't become a playwright overnight. Before he became the famous playwright, director, and producer he is today, he worked at NAPA Auto Parts. In the beginning, his plays didn't sell out like he'd imagined they would, but he kept going because he believed in himself. At one point he ended up homeless, sleeping in his car. Now, he's a household name and owns his own production studio and directs and produces everything from plays to movies. His story is not unique. Look at the life of J.K. Rowling, author of the popular *Harry Potter* series. She was a single mother on welfare. Years later, J.K. is a millionaire.[13]

Both J.K. Rowling and Tyler Perry, despite their different backgrounds, had something in common. They believed in their work. Despite getting rejection letter after rejection letter from publishers or not selling out shows, they never gave up. J.K. Rowling received twelve rejection letters before *Harry Potter* was accepted by a major publishing company. It took six years after Tyler Perry's first play for him to sell out a theatre. Both of them kept going, even when people didn't believe in their dreams. Tennis champions Serena and Venus Williams, arguably some of the greatest tennis champions of our time, grew up in Compton, California, one of the toughest cities in America. Their father, Richard, had a vision that would one day catapult his two daughters to the forefront of the tennis world. They didn't become champions overnight. He began training them at a very young age. The girls practiced tennis when other kids their age were running around on the playground. They travelled far to become students to the best coaches. They suffered injuries. They sacrificed childhood experiences to become great.

That is what this chapter is all about: becoming a champion by fully operating in your gift, even when others don't believe in your dreams. To become a champion, think about what you want to accomplish and how you can achieve it, and don't fall into the trap of thinking that success happens overnight.

Many of us want the overnight success but not the sleepless nights or the worry of how bills will get paid. Or we simply don't want to put in the time to make our dreams a reality. It's a natural tendency to witness the success of others and put them on a pedestal of perfection. After all, these are people that hold world records in their fields or have achieved incredible success in their occupations. They deserve the titles and awards because they *are* champions in their own right. But when you consider their success, don't forget what your favorite heroes and sheroes had to do to get where they are.

My hope is that you realize there is an untapped champion lying dormant inside you. Just because you haven't been nominated for best actress, your book didn't make it to the *New York Times* Best Seller list, or you were passed up for the team leader position at your company doesn't mean there isn't a champion inside you waiting to be unleashed. Remember, champions don't blossom overnight. It sometimes takes years of hard work and dedication to operate in the fullness of your gift. It is up to you to use all the tools and resources you have to make that happen. If your dream is to publish a book, take a writing class at your local college. If you are tired of getting passed over for the supervisor position at your company, find a mentor in your company, shadow a supervisor, or join organizations within your company to help you improve your management skills.

Each and every one of us, in our innate being, has a desire to be and do more than we are currently doing. What is it that *you* desire? Tap into that and take baby steps toward making it happen. That champion in you needs training, mentoring, and pruning to flourish. Nothing will happen overnight, but I promise you it will happen—with some work. When a champion practices his or her skills, they do it with the belief that they will become great. They don't practice to be in the top one hundred or top twenty. They practice to be number one. I want you to work on your skills so that you can become the champion I know you can be.

Nothing comes for free. You will have to sacrifice to achieve your dreams. There will be times of discouragement and disappointment, but I want to encourage you to never give up. Fight for your dream with everything you have. Remember, we are all on this journey together. We are all sitting in the stands rooting for you, hoping to witness you unleash the greatness within.

Reflection:

Take out a piece of paper or your journal. List three areas where you need to improve your skills so you can unleash your inner champion. Now, list three to five ways you can improve each of those skills. Provide actionable goals you can accomplish and include deadlines.

Now, go out and introduce the world to the new champion of you.

Clean Your House

Letting go means to come to the realization that some people are a part of your history, but not part of your destiny. [14]

— Steve Maraboli

There is something about a vacuum or a dust pan that makes my heart smile. I love a clean home. It helps me to think more clearly and relax. I'll be honest with you, since we've spent the past few chapters together—I hate a dirty house. I am the most uncomfortable and off-balance when my house isn't clean.

I'm more relaxed and creative in a clean environment. When my house isn't clean, I don't feel creative. If I'm really pressed to meet a deadline and don't have time to clean, I will go to the library or write at the park. As you may have guessed, it is important for a writer to practice his or her craft. Therefore, I can't stop writing just because my home isn't clean. I think it's important that writers sit down and write even when we don't feel like writing. It can be anything: a poem, a short story, or any other small piece of work.

There have been numerous times when I didn't feel inspired, but I knew I needed to write. I eventually realized I could not focus on my creativity because I kept thinking about the clutter. The clutter in my home was cluttering my brain. It was causing confusion and interrupting my concentration. When I can't find my notes or a certain book, I feel overwhelmed and uneasy.

I have learned that in order to feel creative and free to write, I have to start by keeping my house clean. I have a confession to make. (Did you really think this whole chapter would revolve around a junky house? You should know me by now.) This chapter is not just about cleaning up your house. It is about cleaning up any and everything in your life that makes you feel overwhelmed, uneasy, or off-balance.

Anything can weigh you down: a bad marriage, an unexpected job loss, or a toxic friendship. The best way to clean up your life is to learn to set boundaries. If you are working a dead-end job for a horrible boss, it may be time to move on and search for other opportunities. If you find yourself in bad romantic relationships or unhealthy friendships with people who are no good for you, it is definitely time to move on. By remaining in bad relationships you are inviting clutter—also known as drama. These kinds of situations and relationships can be overwhelming and detrimental to your well-being.

If you stay in bad relationships for too long, you will start to become just like the people driving you crazy. It is the same thing as my brain becoming cluttered when my home is cluttered. There are also times when unhealthy friendships (clutter) can distract you from achieving your goals and succeeding in life. Let's take Sue, for example. Sue has been friends with Nancy for several years. In the beginning, Sue didn't notice Nancy's demanding behavior. It wasn't until several years of friendship that Sue noticed that Nancy would get angry with her when she wasn't available. Nancy would also constantly bombard Sue with her many issues, causing Sue to become depressed herself. Sue, being the nice person that she is, didn't recognize these behaviors right away. Even when she did, she let it continue because she didn't want to hurt Nancy's feelings. What do you think will eventually happen to Sue? She's going to become the angry, demanding person that Nancy is. Jim Rohn said it best: "You are the average of the five people you spend the most time with."[15]

For another example, let's look at a lady named Lisa. Lisa and Jennifer had been friends for several years. Lisa started dating a guy who pressured her into occasional drug use. After five years of this, Lisa's occasional use became a full-blown addiction. Jennifer, the loving friend that she is, tries to help Lisa. She lets Lisa stay on her couch when she needs to. She constantly loans Lisa money, and has kept Lisa's children whenever she would get too high to function. She'd do all this despite the fact that Lisa had stolen from and lied to her. Jennifer remains loyal to a fault. Jennifer has done what she thinks any good friend would do, but there comes a time when she has to evaluate how the friendship is affecting her.

Neither of the relationships described above are very healthy. Friendships that don't help you grow, that aren't supportive, and that just take, take, and take are not friendships at all; they're clutter. It is important to remove yourself from these kinds of relationships because you really do become who you hang around.

Anything that doesn't allow the space for goodness and peace, that keeps you stagnant and adds strife to your life, doesn't deserve a place in your life. It is important to evaluate each one of the relationships in your life. If any of them are harmful, then it is time for you to clean house. In an earlier chapter we learned the importance of saying no. That will be a useful skill when cleaning your house and life.

Reflection:

Take out a piece of paper or your journal and write down your answers to the following questions:

- In what areas of your life can you clean house?

- How would taking stock of your relationships and cleaning house benefit you?

- How has *not* cleaning house impacted your life?

- If you have cleaned house, how has it benefited you?

Spend some time reflecting on the relationships in each area of your life and do some spring cleaning. Happy cleaning!

Show Up!

Vulnerability is about showing up and being seen. It's tough to do that when we're terrified about what people might see or think.[16]

— Brene Brown

Living your life as someone other than you who you were created to be is a heavy burden to carry. I know, because this was once my burden. I've met many people over the years who never knew the real me. What none of them realized was that though they were getting a version of me, they never had the chance to meet the whole me. This was especially true in the workplace. The real Chandra is warm, funny, eccentric, and opinionated. Traits that aren't always easily accepted in certain corporate environments. I can recall a few occasions I was told I was too nice to work in the corporate world and that I should be a missionary or a counselor.

However, during my first few years in the corporate world I had supportive leaders who guided me and positioned me for success. They trained me for the next level. I flourished in that environment. However, after relocating a few times and organizational changes, I was moved to other teams. That is when my practice of not showing up began. One former manager in particular wasn't interested in my ideas or opinions; they simply did not matter to him. I would make a suggestion and he would either completely ignore me or he say "Ummm . . ." and then not answer me. This man shut down every suggestion I had, but when another teammate brought up the very same suggestion, it was a great idea.

At the time, it made me feel small. I felt like my ideas weren't good and

I had nothing to contribute. Instead of growing, I took steps backwards. I no longer felt comfortable speaking up in meetings or expressing my opinion. This very same manager would send the team instant messages telling us exactly what to say during calls with his manager. He deemed it necessary to control everything we did and said, including how many times we said certain words. Yes, you read correctly. He would literally write down the number of times we said certain words and send the list to us. He had an excel spreadsheet to track everybody. I'd never experienced anything like that in my life. I wanted to speak up, but the last time I spoke up about something at work it didn't go so well. So, I stayed silent.

The once bright light I had started to become very dim until it eventually died out completely. My engagement level also suffered. I no longer gave 150 percent. To be truthful, I stopped caring about the work.

I didn't want to cause any issues, so I stayed silent. I allowed him to believe that his solutions were always right. Things went smoother for me when I did this. Later on, I discovered that he was just starting out as a manager, and he was trying to find his footing. There I was, bursting with excitement and eager to learn. I had previous management experience, officer titles, and an MBA behind my name. I'd once held his very same officer title. I think I intimated him. Looking back on the experience, I can honestly say I lost a little bit of myself. It required a lot of energy to pretend I didn't have ideas and solutions.

If that wasn't bad enough, I also found myself not showing up with co-workers. I didn't allow myself to be authentic. Don't get me wrong—I got along really great with people. I was told quite often how great of a person I was to work with. But deep down inside, I wondered what my co-workers would think if they saw the real me. Would they still like me if they knew that things came easily to me? Would they still like me if they knew I had dreams and aspirations outside of Corporate America?

These are just a few of the questions I asked myself over and over again. I was so worried about what others thought of me that I neglected to figure out what I thought of me. I was being someone other than who I was created to be, trying to fit in to get along with my peers and my manager. I should have devoted my time to figuring out who I was and letting that part of me shine. Anything other than that was and is unhealthy. Beloveds, any time you pretend to be someone you're not, it takes work. Why put that much work into being someone you weren't created to be?

Think about the actors who spend sixteen hours on set. In each role, they pretend to be someone they are not. In order for the movie or TV show to be believable, the actors will go "into character," as they call it. Some actors have reported that being "in character" can bleed into their personal lives. Imagine playing a dark, demented role. That could be difficult to let go of in your personal life. Well, you are doing the same thing on a daily basis when you are not showing up as the real you; as your authentic self. The only difference between you and the actors on screen is that they are getting paid—sometimes millions of dollars—to be in character. You are paying a much bigger price with your soul. You may not immediately feel the effects of it, but each day you pretend a small part of your soul is chipped away. You owe it to yourself and the world to show up. Send your authentic self, not a fabricated representation of you or a percentage of you.

Reflection:

Take out a piece of paper or your journal. List five areas in your life where you are not showing up as your authentic self. How does looking at that list make you feel? Below the list, write down some practical ideas for how you can show up as your authentic self.

Wake up tomorrow renewed with a fresh attitude. Show up in your job, in your marriage, and for your children. Most importantly, show up for you!

PART III

WALK COURAGEOUSLY

Forgive Yourself

Take a walk through the garden of forgiveness and pick a flower of forgiveness for everything you have ever done. When you get to that time that is now, make a full and total forgiveness of your entire life and smile at the bouquet in your hands because it truly is beautiful. [17]

— Stephen Richards

Raise your hand if you are proud of everything you've ever done in your life. If you raised your hand, then congratulations! You are indeed a rare individual. Most of us, though we may be good, honest, decent people, are not proud of everything we may have done over the course of our lives.

I want you to pause for a moment and think about what you are struggling to forgive yourself for. Are you still trying to cope with the affair you had fifteen years ago? Did you raise your children the best way you could, or did you leave them with your parents to raise? What is that thing (or things) that you are struggling to forgive yourself for?

It is important to be honest. Telling a lie won't serve me or you. It will only hinder you from moving forward. This chapter isn't about my healing; it is about your healing and my desire to see you free yourself.

I have witnessed countless people struggle with all kinds of dysfunctions that stem from pain and regret. Don't let that be you. It is never too late to change. If no one has ever told you, let me be the first to say that when you lie to yourself, you aren't allowing yourself to heal from that which you need healing from. That healing will only come with practicing truth and authenticity. Truth and authenticity can be a measure of health. Truth requires you to acknowledge and confront painful experiences. Living authentically requires you to operate in the truest and highest form of self, not as who others need or want you to be. This is when your beliefs and values are able to flow from the true core of who you are. By not living authentically and pretending to be someone other than who you really are, you are opening the door for stress to enter. My friends, false pretenses can be emotionally and physically draining. This can lead to stress related illnesses. So, ask yourself: Are you healthy? If not, that's okay; you can be healed. Your first step toward healing is to admit that you don't have a healthy relationship with yourself. In order for anything to change, you have to first acknowledge that.

Many years ago, I had an argument with someone that I love and I said some pretty nasty things. Although I eventually apologized to that person, I did not forgive myself for many years. I thought about it every time I looked at them or heard their name. Then one day, I made a choice to forgive myself. I was tired of hurting for my bad choice of words. I realized if they could forgive me, then I could forgive me. After all, they were the recipient of my cruel words. It was at that point that I chose to be free and began to walk in forgiveness. My wish for you is that you are able to experience that same kind of freedom and that you can create an honest and healthy relationship with yourself. I want you to break free from the chains of regret and unforgiveness.

We're all human and it's natural to be mad at yourself sometimes. But what is *not* natural is not forgiving yourself. The regret must stop today. You deserve to live happily, healthily, and authentically. Most importantly, you deserve to forgive yourself.

Reflection:

Take out a piece of paper or your journal and write down your answers to the following questions:

- What three areas of your life, either professional or personal, can you practice forgiveness toward yourself in?

- How would forgiving yourself allow you to have a healthy and honest relationship with yourself?

- If you were to forgive yourself in those areas; what kind of growth would you expect to achieve?

To help with forgiving yourself, say this affirmation to yourself in the mirror every morning:

I am open and allow the space for the universe to forgive me for my mistakes. Today I forgive you for your past, your present, and your future.

Allow a Little Love In

To be fully seen by somebody, then, and be loved anyhow - this is a human offering that can border on miraculous.[18]

— Elizabeth Gilbert

If I had a dime for every time I heard someone say, "I wish I could find someone to spend the rest of my life with," I'd be rich. Don't misunderstand me—it is a basic human need and desire to seek love. The problem arises when people say they want love but push it away when they find it. The sad thing is, people who do this aren't even aware that they are pushing people away. They do this at a subconscious level for various reasons. See an example of the perfection excuse below.

We've all had girlfriends or have been that girl that meets a good man but pushes him away because we have a twisted perception of what love looks like. Many women believe that love is perfection, and if the man doesn't meet those standards of perfection, then we should be done with the relationship. Often, we've dreamed about falling in love ever since we were little girls. Love is the fairy-tale fantasy of being whisked off into the sunset by Prince Charming. What we fail to realize is that love is not perfection. We have this false belief that the man of our dreams will come wrapped in this neat little box with a bow on it. However, no one tells us that after a few years, Prince Charming will sit on the couch wearing the same sweatpants for two or three days straight and refuse to bathe. He'll never lift a finger to clean anything in the house except on holidays when his family comes to visit. He will pretend he's too tired to put the kids to bed or help them with their homework. The list goes on and on.

What I find amazing, though, is how often we overlook the wonderful qualities that Prince Charming has and instead focus on the not-so-great qualities. Although he won't clean his castle, he may be a strong protector of that castle. He will work hard to provide for your household. He will never disrespect you, lay a hand on you, or discourage you from living your dreams. He will be your biggest supporter. Yet, all you see are the dishes in the sink he refuses to wash or the fact that he never helps the kids with their homework. You don't think of the reasons—he's tired because he works sixteen hour days six days a week to support the family. This is where perspective comes in. It's important to consider your perspective when viewing relationships. For example, if you see your Prince Charming as lazy and worthless, then that is what he will be. But if you see the good qualities in him and focus on those, you will begin to see him in a whole new light. You will move from thinking of him as lazy to thinking of him as a hard worker, support system, and encourager.

Next time you get into an argument with your partner, I want you to remove the word "perfection" from your vocabulary. It simply does not exist. Although your partner may be a good man or woman, they will never be able to meet your strict requirements. Stop requiring them to be perfect and stop basing your love on what they do around the house. Instead, learn to love them as they are and cut them some slack. Remember the six months of Friday nights when you left your partner with three screaming kids so you could go out drinking with your girlfriends for salsa or line dancing night? Remember all the times you told your sister how he or she had gotten on your nerves, and then she gave them the evil eye at the Thanksgiving table and made them feel uncomfortable in their own home? I bet you forgot about all those things, didn't you? I know I did. Well, know that your partner has forgiven you already.

Stop seeking perfection from your partner and just allow him to love you as he is. When you do, you will experience one of the most remarkable feelings ever.

If the perfection excuse doesn't resonate with you, let's explore example number two: the fatherless syndrome. Have you ever met a woman that didn't grow up with a father? You may have noticed that, as a result, she doesn't necessarily know how to accept love. You know, the kind of girl who lashes out in anger at everyone and seeks the attention of men who also have twenty other women on speed dial. She copes with fearing that her partner will abandon her, just like her father did, by pushing men away. Not because anything is wrong with the man, but because she's waiting for him to leave. So she never gets close and never gives him her heart because she isn't expecting him to stay. I was once one of those girls. At the time I was okay with it because, after all, I *was* in the top five in his phone, and that made me special. Does any of this sound familiar to you? Or am I the only one that has ever done this? If that isn't hitting home for you, let me ask you this: Have you ever told anyone you love them? Does it make you uncomfortable to tell a family member, friend, or partner that you love them? And if so, why do you think that is? I'll tell you why—it is because you are afraid to let some love in. I get it; love can be scary and exciting at the same time. However, none of us can exist without love. Love is what makes this world go round. Why would you ever want to deny yourself the right to love?

Reflection:

Take out a piece of paper or your journal and write down your answers to the following questions:

- Do you find it difficult to tell others you love them?

- When was the last time you told someone you loved them?

- How does it make you feel when you say, "I love you"? What kind of feelings and emotions does it provoke to say it out loud?

- Have you been guilty of pushing your partner away for fear that the relationship won't last?

- What situation or relationship in your past evokes feelings of abandonment?

- What situation or relationship from your past evokes feelings of anything less than perfection being bad?

A closed heart only has room for hurt, anger, and mistrust. Open your heart and make room for the person who is waiting to love you, respect you, and cherish you.

Trust Yourself

***Follow your instincts. That's where true wisdom manifests itself.*[19]**

— Oprah Winfrey

Have you ever met someone that you didn't trust the minute you met them? The babysitter you interviewed to watch your children? The man you went on a date with last week who was a narcissist? Or have you ever been asked to collaborate on a project with a co-worker that made you uncomfortable because you thought they might throw you under the bus? Or maybe you met someone and just felt a tingling and sensed that something wasn't right?

I can honestly answer the above questions with a resounding YES. During my corporate America years, I traveled to other locations from time to time. One particular time I flew out of town to meet my new team. I loved traveling and staying in nice hotels and was looking forward to meeting everyone. I must admit, although I looked forward to meeting the team, I was (and still am) a little on the introverted side, so the thought of meeting my new team made me a little nervous, yet I was optimistic. It was exciting. There we were, from all different parts of the country, gathered in a comfortable setting to meet for the first time. My initial impression was that most of the team seemed nice and approachable, except for one particular teammate, who I will not name. I'll just refer to her throughout the rest of this chapter as the teammate from hell. The minute I met her that warm feeling I got when I met the rest of the team fizzled into something unexplainable. I immediately felt uncomfortable. Now, remember—this is my first time meeting her and I knew nothing about her. But I somehow knew I needed to stay away from her. I couldn't quite put my finger on what was wrong, but I knew I felt extremely uncomfortable being around her. This is the part of the story where you may expect me to say I was wrong . . . but that isn't about to happen. I hate to say this, but my initial feelings were absolutely right. She became my enemy, even though we were on the same team.

Within my first week on the team, she went above her boss's head and contacted my manager directly to say I should be fired and shouldn't be a part of their team, despite the fact that her department was the one that recruited me. This kind of behavior went on for at least two years. Unfortunately for me, my manager at the time was also new to the team and didn't know how to nip this behavior in the bud, or just didn't care. Whatever her reasoning, she allowed it to go on. It became so bad that it caused a lot of tension for the entire team. After a few years, she was done torturing me, but unfortunately, she just started targeting the newest person on the team. It was as if she had to put you through an initiation period to prove something. Eventually, she was moved to another team. I later discovered she exhibited this irrational behavior toward other members of her new team as well.

During our initial meeting, I had no idea that for the next two years she would make my life a living hell at work. Yet, the moment I met her, my stomach churned. There was a feeling in my gut, a knowing, that told me to stay away.

Maybe you can't relate to the teammate from hell, maybe instead you are slowly becoming besties with a woman at your local gym. She's friendly, kind, and is always there when you need a shoulder to cry on. Unbeknownst to you, she is spreading your business around the entire neighborhood. It's not intentional, she's not a malicious person, but she can't seem to keep a secret. Girlfriend loves to gossip. You knew the moment you met her that she was offering up a little too much information, but you brushed it off instead of paying closer attention. You ignored your initial feelings about her because you were lonely and needed a friend. Is any of this ringing a bell for you? Are you sitting on the couch right now saying, "Girl, yes, I've been there too"?

Well, let me ask you: How did that work out for you? You ignored your gut feeling about her, and now you are the talk of the neighborhood. I'll bet that the fact that you didn't listen to your gut and stop sharing your personal business with her made you feel like crap.

Both stories are examples of how our gut speaks to us. However, it is up to us to listen. We do ourselves a disservice when we ignore our gut and put more trust in the other person than we have in ourselves. It breaks my heart to see people that can't trust themselves. After all, the one person you should be able to trust is YOU!

Let me wrap up by saying that there will be times when people enter our lives to teach us a lesson, whether it's to make us stronger or teach us about ourselves. That's okay; I see it as a part of our journey. As God, the Universe, teaching us the lessons that will help define and shape who we are. It's the universe stepping up to meet you with your greatest need. If you have difficulty trusting yourself, you will meet someone who will allow you the opportunity to strengthen that muscle.

The issue is when there is a sustained continual practice of not trusting your gut. Like anything else in life, to get better at it, you have to use it. Your gut is just like any other muscle in your body—when you use it, you are strengthening it. In order to improve your trust in yourself, you will have to test it through experiences and situations that require you to test that trust. For example: If you're faced with the decision of whether or not to take a new job in a new state, even if the pay is much more than what you're making, you need to trust your gut and ask, "Is this the right decision? Should I stay where I am?" When you meet the man who you believe is the "one," but your gut says he's not the one for you, will you continue to date him because you want to be in a relationship so desperately, or will you leave the relationship?

Your power lies in trusting yourself and knowing that each decision you make is the best decision at that moment for your life. Can I ask you something? If you're uncomfortable and a tad bit unsure of your decisions, why would you expect others to trust you? Imagine how wonderful it will feel when you walk away from a situation trusting that you made the best decision for you. Despite not having all the facts, you trusted yourself when something didn't feel right with your gut and you walked away unharmed. That is what trusting yourself is all about—making an informed (gut) decision even if you don't have all the information (facts). I promise you there will never be a time in your life when you will regret trusting yourself. However, there will be times when you will have to wrestle with the regret of not trusting yourself.

Reflection:

Take out a piece of paper or your journal and write down your answers to the following questions:

- What areas in your life are you struggling with trusting yourself in? How can you start to trust yourself more?

- What does trusting in yourself look and sound like to you?

- Think back over your life. Has there ever been a time when you didn't trust yourself but demanded that others trust you?

I dare you to begin to trust yourself, your decisions, and your thoughts—immediately.

Be Honest with Yourself

When I was being honest with myself, I had to own that there was something about me that was drawing an energy in my life that left me feeling underserved and unfulfilled. I decided to grow. I decided to purge myself of anyone and anything that was not full of goodness, serving me or making me happy.[20]

— Niecy Nash

This was one of the most difficult chapters in this book to write because it forced me to confront one of my biggest struggles: being disloyal to myself and feeding myself lies. I did this a lot when it came to friendships and dating.

When I would lie to myself, I knew it wasn't right. My gut and every part of my being told me that what I was practicing would ultimately cost me more than it was worth; it would cost me my soul. Yet I continued on that destructive path because I longed for something more. As a result, I found myself depressed and contemplating suicide. I now understand that the "more" was a longing for love and connection.

My single mother spent most of her time working so that we could have the basic necessities in life. She did the best she could with the resources she had. At a young age, I realized that my mother was the strong, silent type. She was and still is a woman of few words.

Looking back, I believe my unhealthy relationships stemmed from my family unit. My mom was quiet and never explained how relationships worked or what to look for in a man or in friendships. My dad, on the other hand, just wasn't around very much to have those conversations with. I really believe that was the catalyst that helped push me into unhealthy relationships. I never saw an example of what a healthy one looked like. Therefore, I sought friendships and romantic relationships with people as unhealthy as I was.

As far back as my childhood, I recall being drawn to slightly misguided girls like myself. Some wanted to have children at the tender age of fourteen because they yearned for someone to love. Many of them didn't feel like anyone loved them and thought they would find that love in a child. Others looked to sexual relationships for love and connection. I never desired to have a child at a young age, nor was I sexually active, but I did find myself heading in the wrong direction as I grew older. As I began to date, I found that I was attracted to men who were emotionally unavailable. I accepted this because I didn't want to be in a serious relationship at the time. What I didn't realize until years later was that *I* was emotionally unavailable. That explained why I sought unavailable men.

My self-esteem was so low that I was willing to stay in these relationships to have some type of love and connection. I lied to myself just to be with these men. I would tell myself that how they treated me was okay because if they left me, no one else would want me. Although I looked beautiful on the outside (by society's standards), on the inside I was a hot mess.

This was a familiar pattern in most of my relationships for a few years, but as I got older, something strange happened. I became more in tune with myself. I started to declare that I deserved more. That I was worthy of more in friendships and in romantic relationships. I was tired of hurting. I was tired of pushing people away that really did love me. I grew up and realized my worth. I became tired of lying to myself about what friendship and love looked like. Instead of ignoring the fact that I was spending time with a friend who sucked the life out of me and was with a man I saw no future with, I faced those situations head-on and released those toxic people from my life. Friendship shouldn't drain you. Love shouldn't be hurtful.

Maybe your lie has nothing to do with unhealthy relationships. Maybe you tell yourself that you have to be perfect because you are the only woman in a managerial position in your office. Or maybe you tell yourself that you are financially stable, but really you are buried in credit card debt. There are many ways that we lie to ourselves. For years I kept finding myself in unhealthy relationships. Fear of being alone and lacking love and connection was a major driving force keeping me in those relationships. Fear of hurting the other person's feelings was the other force keeping me in those relationships. I now realize that I didn't care about myself enough to be honest with myself.

Thank goodness I discovered my greatness. I shed pounds of low self-esteem and gained a lot of greatness weight. Gaining that weight was one of the best things that ever happened to me. I stopped lying to myself and started telling myself the truth of how wonderful and magnificent I was. Oh, and let me tell you, honey—this weight loss looks good on me, and it feels good too. I want the same for you. My hope is that you recognize how precious you are and realize that you deserve more than to be in the company of a liar, even if that liar is you.

The examples mentioned above are just a few of the ways that I have been less than honest with myself. But each of those experiences, as difficult as they were, taught me a lesson. A very tough lesson: that as difficult as it was to walk away from each of those relationships, it was harder to look myself in the mirror every day knowing that I wasn't being true to myself and putting my needs first. After all, I knew the relationships weren't going to work out, but I was so desperate for love and attention that I hurt the most important person: me. I can write this chapter with such conviction because I've spent many days consciously being honest with myself.

It's not always easy to recognize when you aren't being honest with yourself. The lie can be blatant or like a pimple hidden beneath the surface that will eventually rear its ugly head.

There are many ways we lie to ourselves every day. By lying to yourself, you are doing yourself a great disservice. Your lies will eventually catch up with you, and often show up at the most inconvenient times. The lie will show up as low self-esteem when you meet the man of your dreams and run him away because you acted like a complete basket case. Or it will show up when you're trying to figure out how to move forward in life. It might show up on a conference call at work. We have no control over when that lie will show up, but trust me—it always will. To avoid the headache and embarrassment later, learn to deal with it now. Call it out on the carpet for what it is: a lie. Be brave and speak your truth.

Reflection:

Take out a piece of paper or your journal and write down your answers to the following questions:

- What lies are you telling yourself on a daily basis? Be honest. This is your chance to call that lie out on the carpet. See it for what it is: a story that you tell yourself over and over in the hopes of convincing yourself and others that it is the truth.

- How could your life be better if you spoke your truth?

- What steps can you start taking immediately to practice your truth?

Practice your truth and be honest with yourself every day, starting today.

Let It Go!

Reflect upon your present blessings, of which every man has many—not on your past misfortunes, of which all men have some. [21]

— **Charles Dickens**

Do you sometimes worry too much? Have you ever lost sleep at night due to that worrying? You are not alone. Approximately 48 percent of people in the United States reported lying awake at night due to stress, and sleep deprivation is the number seven cause of stress.[22] We all have been or will be stressed in our lives. We all worry about how the bills will get paid, about job stability, or about our kids.

I've discovered that how we react to situations is what causes us to be stressed. Have you ever met someone (or maybe that someone is you) that refuses to let go of the past? They will hold on to it for dear life. You know, the person that constantly says they wish they would or could have done things differently. We've all been that person or dealt with that person. There were times in my life when I made myself physically sick thinking about all the things I should have done differently. Guess what—I didn't do them differently, and I'm still the woman I am today despite all the mistakes I've made. My life, at one point, seemed like a series of bad decisions. I now understand that every experience, good and bad, was preparing me for now; for my future. Preparing me to be the author, poet, and motivational speaker I am today. That's right. Each one of my experiences gave me the motivation and inspiration to speak and write; not to mention the subject material to speak and write about.

When I finally realized that the past is impossible to change, I made a critical decision to stop beating myself up over it. I began to focus my energy on more positive things, like practicing gratitude. I started off simple in the beginning. I thanked God for food, for shelter, and even for my breath as I woke up each morning. As I continued to operate in the gratitude space, I had less room to focus on the mistakes I made. You may think I'm crazy for this one, but I decided to have a funeral for my negative thoughts. I literally gave myself a date to grieve, and at the end of that day, I said—out loud—"Chandra, I don't want to hear any more about this subject. Let It Go! These negative thoughts are not here to serve you, so why are you allowing them room to grow in your life?" I began to surrender to the power of my future and suffocated my past. Letting the past go has felt so amazing and powerful. I recommend having your own funeral for your negative thoughts where you surrender to your future. It will help you to experience the power of your amazing self!

Reflection:

Take out a piece of paper or your journal and write down your answers to the following questions:

- What are you holding on to that you need to let go of?

- How is holding on to this hurting you?

- How is it impacting your relationships with others?

- What would your life look like if you finally let it go?

Now have a funeral for it, and let it go.

Fight the Fear

***One of the greatest discoveries a man makes,
one of his great surprises, is to find he can
do what he was afraid he couldn't do.*** [23]

— Henry Ford

The definition of fear is a "distressing emotion aroused by impending danger, evil, pain, etc. Whether the threat is real or imagined; the feeling or condition of being afraid."[24]

The key line I want to point out in that definition is "whether the threat is real or imagined." Yes, there will be times in our lives when we'll have fear and it is justified. For example, imagine you're hiking in the woods and stumble across a bear. Or walking to your car late at night when a stranger approaches. These are examples of healthy fear. In each of these instances, fear is good for us. Fear, in the right situation, is healthy. It can signal we're in danger. It is the body's response to a threat. It is the fight or flight response.

However, fear can be unhealthy sometimes. Let's say you have an upcoming test, but instead of studying for it, you sit at home for a week stressed out about whether you'll pass it. No good can come from that. It would have been a much better use of time to spend that week studying. People often spend months focusing on what can go wrong instead of putting together an action plan to ensure their success.

Those habits come from a fear of failure. There are many kinds of fear, and not everyone is afraid of the same thing. Yet, there is one thing that is universal when it comes to fear: if fear is allowed to fester in one's life, it can be debilitating. Fear left unchecked will keep you from moving forward. It is the reason so many talented and gifted people are living unfulfilled lives. They aren't following their passions because of fear. I knew an amazing, talented woman who was an excellent artist. Yet right now, she's working as a cashier at a retail shop. She loved art and loved drawing, but she wasn't able to move past her fear. Being afraid is natural. It takes great strength to be afraid but move forward anyway. This is called pushing past the fear. What many people don't realize is that fear is manageable. How do you manage it, you might ask? It's simple. The first thing you must do is acknowledge it. Have you ever heard of the saying "You can't change something you don't acknowledge"? Well, it's true. When you acknowledge something, you take the first step toward healing. Which brings me to step number two: visualization. Visualize the thing you are afraid of. If that is public speaking, picture yourself standing in the front of a crowded room giving a successful talk. Visualize this over and over until it becomes your reality. The next step is to focus on the positive outcome. Step number four is to plan. That's right. Make a plan that will ensure your success. If you are afraid of speaking in public and your goal is to overcome it, then your action plan might look like this:

Goal: Give a speech in public
Deadline: December 31, 2017
Action steps:
- Join a speaking club by October 1, 2017
- Find a mentor by October 15, 2017
- Give first practice speech by October 20, 2017
- Give second practice speech by October 30, 2017
- Give third practice speech by November 15, 2017
- Give presentation at work by December 15, 2017

Can you imagine how gratifying it would feel to finally give that work presentation? It *is* possible—if you follow the steps above. Before you know it, we'll all be saying "Congratulations my friend, you did it!" You were afraid of public speaking, but you did it anyway.

These steps to conquer fear can be used in just about every situation. No matter what you're facing, always remember you can overcome it by acknowledging it, visualizing yourself doing it, focusing on a positive outcome, and putting a plan together and executing that plan despite your fear. If you follow those four steps, you are guaranteed to win. I know because I've used them in my own life.

Reflection:

Take out a piece of paper or your journal and write down your answers to the following questions:

- What are you afraid of? List five examples.

- How have these fears manifested in your life?

- What has fear stopped you from doing?

- Have you ever taken any steps to conquer your fears?

- How do you think you'll feel when you stop allowing fear to keep you from moving forward?

Select one fear you would like to overcome from your list above. Use the four-step plan discussed in this chapter to overcome it. Now go out and conquer your fear.

PART IV

ACCESS YOUR POWER

Conduct Daily Check-Ins

***Self-compassion is simply giving the same kindness
to ourselves that we would give to others.***[25]

— Christopher Germer

I used to think I had to do daily check-ins with my friends. That's what good friends do, right? A good friend will laugh with you, have your back when necessary, loan you a dime when you only have a penny, and be that emotional support that is so often missing in relationships these days. This made it easy for me to pick up the phone to check on my friends daily and ask, "Hey girl, how are the kids, are they still acting crazy?" "Is hubby going to let you buy that house?" "How is work going? Is your boss still micromanaging you?" We've all had these types of conversations with our friends.

There is absolutely nothing wrong with checking in with your friends. The problem arises when you are spending all your time checking in with your friends and none of that time checking in with yourself. Hear me out. No one knows you better than you, and if you aren't willing to check in with your feelings and needs, no one else will.

Women are especially nurturing, which makes it easy to worry about our friends or family members and forget to take care of ourselves. But it's important to make a course correction and check-in with ourselves when we start to feel that way. Trust me, you will be surprised at how much more fulfilled you will feel after each check-in. Checking in with yourself puts you in touch with your feelings. It will also help you to determine how life is treating you. Don't you want to know if you are happy? If you're settling for less in life? Have you thought about what is next for you in your career or your personal relationships? These types of thoughts lead to personal development. Personal development is not just about writing down your goals, though that is a part of it.

It's about getting to know the person you are today so you can become the person you want to be tomorrow.

You can't become who you want to be if you don't know who you are. I encourage you to spend some time figuring out who you are. Nurture that woman that stands before you every day. Check in with her to find out how she's doing. I promise you, she will thank you for it.

Reflection:

Ask yourself these questions:

- How did today go?

- How do I feel?

- Is there anything I need to do differently, the same, or more of?

Make it a daily practice to check in with *you*.

Actively Participate in Your Growth

Without continual growth and progress, such words as improvement, achievement, and success have no meaning.[26]

— Benjamin Franklin

Years ago, I received some great advice from a former manager. To sum up the conversation, she told me I could go as far as I wanted within the organization, but that it was all up to me. I learned then that no one will hand you a promotion. You have to work hard, attend training, volunteer for assignments, and network. That conversation stuck with me for many years. I used to believe that I would get noticed if I simply worked hard, if I was nice to my co-workers and management. But I quickly learned that being liked wasn't enough.

I had to show my willingness to adapt to changes, to network, to excel at my job, and continually improve through training—all at the same time. It's not enough to just sit idly by; you must be an active participant in your own growth. I couldn't expect my supervisor to tap me on the shoulder or select me for a job promotion if I didn't show interest, if I wasn't a leader, and if I wasn't actively learning new things. You getting the picture? I eventually realized that the same lesson applied to my personal life.

Do you ever think about doing something different, but find yourself spending more time thinking about it than actually doing it? Have you ever sat at your desk wishing your school loan debt would go away? Did it magically go away? Chances are, it probably didn't. What if I told you making your student loan debt disappear is not impossible? But you have to work at it. First, you need to create a budget. The budget must include expenses, income, and a timeline for paying down the debt. It may mean you have to get rid of the two hundred dollar cable bill for a year, or start bringing your lunch to work every day, or cut down on getting a manicure every week. The point is, it can be done. The success of your plan is determined by the type of plan you put together and how focused you remain on executing it. How many of you reading this want to lose weight? Now, how successful do you think you would be if you ate ice cream every night and pizza for breakfast every day? You'd have more success putting together a healthy meal plan and an exercise routine—and sticking to it. This is what I refer to as "actively participating in your growth." Don't wait until Uncle Sam decides to lower your school loan interest rate or sit by hoping that you'll somehow lose the weight one day. One day won't happen until you *make* it happen. What are you willing to do today to make "one day" a reality?

Reflection:

Choose from one or more areas below where you could stand to be more active in your personal development:

- Financial

- Spiritual

- Personal Development

- Health

- Relationships

Beside each area, list three ways you will actively participate in your growth, and include deadlines with your goals.

Indulge in Self-Discovery

People often say that this or that person has not yet found himself. But the self is not something one finds, it is something one creates.[27]

— Thomas Szasz

You've probably heard these phrases many times: self-reflection, self-discovery, and taking a little "me" time. But do you actually practice what these phrases say? I know it sounds like a bunch of hoopla that someone made up to make lots of money, but it's not. These practices actually work. There is power in self-discovery and spending time in reflection. These two activities are part of the daily check-in process that we talked about a few chapters ago. I know the importance of self-discovery because I've put it into practice and benefitted from it.

I didn't always love myself, something proven by some of the less-than-ideal decisions I've made over the years. What I discovered is, when I got to know me, there was no way I *couldn't* love myself. I wish I could tell you it was an overnight process, but it wasn't. In fact, I've spent many years working on self-discovery and reflection. It's a lifetime journey, but the process is just as valuable as the destination. By embarking on the journey, you'll discover the gem you truly are on the inside. So, I'm here to tell you it's not a bunch of crap. This stuff really works.

Through self-discovery, I was able to improve my self-esteem and see how beautiful I am. On the outside, yes, but more importantly, I realized how beautiful my heart is. I was able to recognize how much I light up at the thought of other people finding their joy and how much I enjoyed helping them discover it. That's why I became a philanthropist and began volunteering my time and money. How can that not be beautiful? Most importantly, I realized I am God's child. Even though I will never be a size two or weigh 115 pounds again, I can recognize how wonderful I am with my kinky hair and how great I look in my size eight or ten jeans, hips, butt, and all. I know I'm beautiful because God loves me just the way I am, and that means I have no choice but to love me for exactly who I am as well.

Self-discovery has allowed me to recognize the things that bring me peace. Over the past several years, I've spent many blissful days in nature journaling, practicing yoga, walking in the park, and sitting in front of the lake near my home. This quiet time has truly been a gift for me. It has allowed me to kill the noise from everyday stressors and focus on me. I stopped focusing on work, my marriage, my family, and I selfishly focused on me. I thought about why I was here on this earth. I asked myself questions like: What are my values? What is my purpose? How can I help others to achieve their dreams? Why was I chosen to do the work of helping others?

I discovered that childhood holds the key to many of life's questions. I grew up in poverty so I could have the drive to dig my way out of it. I worked three jobs to pay for college. As difficult as that was, it taught me to have empathy for people who can't afford college. If I did not have that experience, then I would have never established a scholarship almost ten years ago to help deserving students pay for college.

Even though I've had many difficult days in my life, I understand that those days were part of my journey toward fulfilling my ultimate goal, which is to empower women to live happier and more fulfilling lives. And after the worst moments of battling life-threatening depression, I literally rebuilt myself from the ground up.

What I love about self-discovery is how powerful and transformational it is. As I was in the process of editing this chapter, I came across an article in the *Huffington Post* that likened self-discovery to spring cleaning of the mind, emotions, relationships, and surroundings. That is a unique and transparent way of defining it. The article went on to describe finding your purpose in life. It suggested digging deep into your childhood and discovering the experiences that helped to shape you and your beliefs.[28]

As I glanced through the article, I was relieved to discover that I had been on the right path all along. I wish I could tell you that the journey of self-discovery is easy, but it's not. However, anything worth having will require some work. Self-discovery *is* a lot of work, but if done the right way, it can be life-changing and incredibly positive. It will require you to be honest and transparent with yourself. You must be willing to open yourself up to YOU. The only requirement is that you must be willing to get to know you. Along the journey, you will learn some things about yourself that you don't like. Maybe your values are out of alignment with how your parents raised you. Maybe you're not being true to your core. Or maybe you're not doing the work that you were called to do. This is a big reason that many of us suffer in silence, feeling like something just isn't right in our lives but not able to put our finger on it.

I always hear people say they want to meet someone and get married one day. They spend most of their life daydreaming about this fairy-tale Prince Charming.

They meet a guy and go out on a date, only to leave the date or relationship, feeling unfulfilled. Well, this can happen for several reasons. Maybe that person just wasn't the person for you. Or maybe that person had some great qualities, but you couldn't see those qualities because you were so wrapped up in the fairy-tale Prince that you've dreamed about for years. This may make you uncomfortable, but I've never been one to sugarcoat anything. I believe that if we truly care about each other, we must learn to speak the truth to each other.

You cannot and will not grow if you don't know.

In some cases, the reason you aren't in a relationship is because you aren't ready for one yet. Maybe you still have a lot of work to do on yourself. Here is where self-discovery comes into play. If you don't know who you are, what your beliefs are, what you will stand for, what you're looking for, and what makes you happy, how can you expect a man to fill a hole that you have on the inside? I'm here to tell you that no man can fill that void.

My beloveds, self-discovery isn't for your partner or your family—it's for you. You may not like everything you see. You may realize you suck as a best friend, that you're a horrible boss, or that you're selfish or unreliable. But how can you change if you are unwilling to do the work to find out exactly who you are? In the end, you will walk away after discovering yourself feeling fulfilled. You'll have purpose and intention. You owe it to yourself to be the version of you that you were created to be, and it starts with self-discovery.

Reflection:

Invest some time—today—to discover who you are. Take out a piece of paper or your journal and write down a mission statement for your life. Then, think about the questions below and write down your answers.

- Do you know why you were created?

- Do you know what your purpose is?

- How are you going to discover your purpose?

- What are your values and beliefs?

- How has your childhood shaped you into the person you are today?

- How can self-discovery help you to become more fulfilled and happier?

After you have honestly answered the questions, reflect on what important lessons you have learned about yourself. Begin on your journey of self-discovery today and find out who you can become tomorrow.

Give Yourself a Hug

You yourself, as much as anybody in the entire universe, deserve your love and affection.[29]

— **Buddha**

I was having a very engaging conversation with a healing coach one day when she began to speak about the power of hugging yourself. She talked about how the simple act of wrapping your arms around your chest can evoke self-love. As we continued the conversation, she asked me if I made it a habit to hug myself. I shyly replied that I had in the past, but it wasn't something that I'd done recently. Right then and there, a lightbulb went off in my head. We hug friends, family, co-workers, and sometimes even strangers, filling them up with doses of love. Through a hug, we can leave them with all these amazing feelings like safety, protection, security, and love. All the things we need in our own lives, but we don't take the time to fill ourselves up with those healing hugs.

You need to know you are emotionally safe with yourself. I encourage you to make it a daily practice to fill yourself up with safety, protection, security, and love by giving yourself a hug. You are worthy of these things— and so much more. Don't sit idly by waiting for someone else to give them to you. Give them to yourself. You need to know you are loved.

I'm going to break tradition for this chapter. Instead of asking you to reflect on a set of questions, I'm offering you an affirmation.

Affirmation:

Make this commitment to yourself. Start by reading the following sentence, inserting your name where indicated. A good way to remind yourself to say it is by writing it down and posting it on your wall or in a space where it is visible at all times.

I, [insert name here], am worthy of all good things. I am worthy of safety, protection, and security. Most importantly, I am worthy of love from me.

Now go hug yourself. ☺

Tie the Knot

To love oneself is the beginning of a lifelong romance.[30]

— Oscar Wilde

For several years I subscribed to the belief that a person should date themselves. Dating is fun. It's a chance to get to know someone or expand your horizons. It can be exciting and nerve-wracking all at the same time, especially if you're not the adventurous kind but your date is. And if it's someone you are really excited to get to know, you will most likely get those pre-date butterflies in your stomach.

Date night can look different to different people. For some, it is a night on the couch with your favorite movie. For others, it is a visit to a museum or park. You get the point. When you are dating, you can pick any place to enjoy. If it's a really good date, by the end of the evening you will be eager to go on the next date. What is important isn't where you go, but the quality of the time you spend together. Let's expand this concept of going on a date with someone. Think about those butterflies in your stomach I referenced a few sentences ago. Now, imagine having those same butterflies at the thought of spending time with yourself. Can you imagine being excited to take a walk around the park or to take yourself out on a lunch date, getting to know yourself?

You should know me well enough by now to know I would not suggest anything I haven't done myself. Although I am not single, I still take myself out on dates because it is important that I have a solid relationship with myself. It is important to me that my identity doesn't revolve around my spouse. I know who I am with him and without him. No offense is meant to him, and he knows this. I enjoy going to museums alone. I never get tired of taking myself to the movies or walking around the park. I truly believe in the importance of spending time with myself.

While I still believe in the concept of dating yourself, I've since expanded that to marrying yourself. Let me explain why. When we date people, there isn't always a commitment, especially in the beginning of the relationship. You're spending time together, trying to get to know each other and decide whether this is the person you'd like to eventually settle down with. Sometimes during that process there isn't a sense of commitment. Either party can walk away from the relationship at any time. But when you marry someone there is commitment, there is unity, and there is the kind of love that says, "No matter what, I'm going to be here with you. We may experience difficult times. We may not always agree. But we are in this together." That is the level of dedication required for a marriage to be successful. Now, why would we have that level of dedication to someone else and not to ourselves? Do you see where I'm going with this? I want you to experience that level of commitment to yourself. It is an absolute joy to be able to make that kind of promise and commitment to yourself.

When you make that kind of commitment to yourself, you will attract people that see how much value you place on yourself, and who will treat you with that same level of respect. So, I say forget dating and tie the knot with yourself.

Affirmation:

Say the following out loud, inserting your name where indicated.

I [insert name here] promise to love, honor, and obey my self, forsaking all others. Through sickness and in health, for richer or for poorer. I am committed to this relationship with myself.

Start every morning by standing in front of your mirror and saying your vows out loud to yourself.

PART V
STAND BOLDLY

Let Your Little Light Shine

If only you could sense how important you are to the lives of those you meet; how important you can be to people you may never even dream of. There is something of yourself that you leave at every meeting with another person. [31]

— **Fred Rogers**

We've come so far on this journey together. Therefore, it should not come as a surprise to you that I am going to ask another hard question to get your brain cells moving. Who are you? What makes you unique? I want you to really be truthful when answering these two questions. Think about your answers, because they will set you up for the lesson in this chapter. It is important that we define and discover who we are. I believe in purposeful creation, or the idea that we are all created for a purpose. Otherwise, we would not have been born. When you discover who you are and what your purpose is, you have a duty to share it with others. This is called service to mankind.

Who are you? What is your purpose? What gifts do you have that the world is waiting for you to unleash? Do people often tell you how kind, caring, analytical, organized, or nurturing you are? Well, we could use more kind, caring, analytical, organized, and nurturing people in this world. Whether you are serving as a mentor to young people, on a ministry at church, or volunteering to teach a local community class on budgeting and finance, it is important to use your gift. Don't ever think that you can't do something because others are doing it. There are millions of volunteers and mentors, but they are not you. You have something that is unique: you.

Never forget that there is always a space in this world for you to operate in your gift. However, the million-dollar question is: Are you using your gifts to serve others, or are you letting them lie dormant?

For years I was told how caring, helpful, and nurturing I was. Many people said that I should mentor young people, write books, or become a life coach. It wasn't until a few years ago that I started making plans to make some of those things come true. Although I've always dreamed of writing, I didn't know how to make that a reality. Instead of working diligently toward my goal, I hid behind excuse after excuse. One of my favorite excuses had to do with not wanting others to know that I had these talents or hobbies. Growing up in my era, to be cool you were either a hip-hop junkie or wanted to be a singer or a rapper. I, on the other hand, thoroughly enjoyed reading and writing.

Oh, how times have changed. I'm no longer embarrassed about my love of reading. Reading is therapeutic for me. It takes me to foreign lands and into the lives of characters I may never have had the chance to meet. I get to live vicariously through the characters in these books and I get to lead many exciting lives. I love every minute of it.

"A reader lives a thousand lives before he dies . . . The man who never reads lives only one."[32]
— *George R.R. Martin*

What is it about yourself that you are afraid to let others know? Are you afraid to let them see the real you, the person you are at your core? Are you afraid of showing that part of you that you close off from the world? Honey, let me save you a lot of stress and headaches by sharing something

I wish someone would have shared with me a long time ago: Your survival in this world depends on you being comfortable in your own skin. Being comfortable in your authenticity. This means that you must let whatever you desire in life, or who you are deep down at your core, shine. Don't dim your light for fear of how you'll be perceived. You're doing both yourself and this world a disservice. The world is waiting on the gifts that God has given you. You need to share them with us.

Do you remember a few chapters ago when we talked about showing up? Believe it or not, there is a natural order or progression of things when it comes to that topic. First, you have to release any type of fear that you are holding on to. Next, you have to *show up*. Once you've conquered the fear, then it's time for you to show up and let your little light shine. It takes boldness. It takes a brave woman to let her light shine. It takes commitment to show up in the workplace and showcase your skills and talents. It takes strength to show up at home for yourself, for your kids, and for your husband. Let your light shine. Don't just show up occasionally—show up every time you walk into a room.

If you're a business owner, show up in your business. If you're an employee, show up at your company. If you belong to an organization or group, show up there too. Guess what? Your life has nothing to do with you and everything to do with your calling and purpose. You have a duty to let your light shine. When you let it shine, you give others permission to let theirs shine; and who knows, your services or your products may be the answer that someone needs. Happy shining!

Reflection:

Take out a piece of paper or your journal and write down your answers to the following questions:

- What gifts are lying dormant in you that are just waiting to be unleashed?

- How are you making your life better by dimming your light?

- Who might benefit if you let your light shine?

Don't hold back. Now go out and let your light shine!

Embrace Your Uniqueness

When you're different, sometimes you don't see the millions of people who accept you for what you are. All you notice is the person who doesn't.[33]

— Jodi Picoult

Ever since I was a little girl I've felt different. Although to the naked eye I looked just like other little girls my age, deep down on the inside I wasn't, and I knew it. After all, I was a little black girl from the projects who loved classical music and film. If that isn't considered unique I don't know what is.

I could even go so far as to say that I always felt like the normal people of the world operated in one bubble and that I was operating in a completely different bubble. My bubble wasn't cool, it wasn't interesting, it was just . . . there. In my bubble—also known as my world—there was a lot of poetry writing and daydreaming about traveling the world.

In contrast, most of my classmates were concerned with having kids, selling drugs, or having sex. Yes, they were planning to have kids at the tender age of fourteen and fifteen because it was "cute" to have someone look like them. Having a baby never even crossed my mind. In my opinion, it was absurd to think I could take care of a child when I couldn't take care of myself.

How many of you have ever operated in your own bubble? If you have, you know how isolating it can be. Although I had friends, I still felt isolated because I knew my bubble was not the same as other people's bubbles. My outside exterior screams corporate and professional, but that is not all there is to me. Deep down I am a creative, artsy person who loves to surround myself with other creatives. Over time I began to grow, and instead of shying away from the things that made me different, I learned to embrace them. I also began looking for people who would embrace and support my uniqueness to surround myself with.

Can I offer you a bit of advice? Who cares what people think? They will always have an opinion. Will you live the rest of your life caring about what other people think, or will you decide once and for all that the only opinion that matters is yours? Deciding that is what it will take to step into the fullness of who you are and embrace your uniqueness. Imagine how freeing it would feel to embrace every part of you, regardless of others' opinions.

Reflection:

Take out a piece of paper or your journal and write down your answers to the following questions:

- What is that thing that sets you apart from others that you aren't willing to acknowledge?

- Why would it be beneficial for you to embrace that part of you?

- What amazing things could you achieve if you learned to embrace your uniqueness?

Give yourself permission to embrace your uniqueness.

Make Confidence Your Best Friend

No one can make you feel inferior without your consent.[34]

— Eleanor Roosevelt

Have you ever witnessed a child dress themselves? If you have, then you know nothing ever matches. One day, on a TV series that features a single mother who happens to be an actress, the mother gives her son permission to dress himself. To my surprise, her son came out of his room with a shirt, shorts, jogging pants, and cowboy boots. In between my hysterical fits of laughter, I managed to hear her ask her son if he was sure he wanted to wear that outfit. He confidently replied, "Yes." At that moment, it occurred to me how confident children can be. Here was this precious little boy willing to walk proudly into a world that can often be critical and harsh. I wish I could say that because he is a child, he is shielded from criticism. However, we live in a time when even kids can be just as harsh and critical as adults. That is why I applauded this young child for standing confidently and boldly in the world. What a brave little young man. Although this was a TV show, it portrayed a real trait that kids have and that is confidence.

Would you have the confidence to leave your home in shorts, jogging pants, and cowboy boots? I know I wouldn't dare leave the house like that. Being completely transparent, I've never put too much thought into how I dress. I was always the kind of girl that would climb trees with my male cousin and play Battleship instead of playing with his sister and her Barbies. This pattern continued into adulthood. My husband and sister constantly tell me I need to go shopping because I will wear the same five jeans in heavy rotation if they're clean. That's all that matters to me: that I'm neat and clean.

Imagine how much happier and freer life would be if you and I had half the guts that this young man had. Most of the time we don't have the confidence we should. Let me share an example with you. On New Year's Eve, 2015, I was sitting at the doctor's office waiting to be seen. I noticed this forty-something-year-old woman with this beautiful purse slung over her wrist. Now, I'm sitting in my seat waiting to be called by the nurse and biding my time staring at this woman's purse, not because I wanted to snatch it, but out of admiration. I love purses. I will leave home with a messy ponytail, ratty t-shirt, and day-old pair of skinny jeans; but I've got to have a really nice purse on my arm. I digress; I smiled at the woman and said, "Excuse me Ms.—I love your purse." She responded, "Oh, this old thing; this purse is so old it doesn't look like nothing." I insisted that I loved it and thought it was beautiful as she continued to tell me how old it is.

It occurred to me in that moment how often we women struggle to accept compliments, myself included. Why do you think that is? What is so wrong with accepting a compliment? I have struggled with this for many years. In my case, I lacked the confidence it took to simply say thank you. I didn't want to appear conceited. So, just like the woman in the doctor's office, I would catch myself saying, "Oh, this ole thing?" Now, I've learned to just shut my trap and take the compliment. I've learned to stop trying to convince others that I am not worthy of a compliment.

One of the differences between a woman who is confident and one who isn't is that when you're confident, you won't diminish a compliment coming your way. You will hold your head high and simply smile and say thank you.

Before we wrap up this chapter, let me be clear about what I mean by "confidence." Confidence doesn't always have to do with your physical appearance, though that is a small part of it. Confidence is really about how you feel on the inside, which translates into the other areas of your life. Are you confident in your skills at work, or do you sit in the back of the room at every team meeting and never express your ideas and opinions? Are you confident in your body, or do you wear big baggy clothes to cover up your hips and butt because you think it looks disgusting? Are you confident in your relationship, or are you constantly checking his cell phone to see if he's still talking to his ex? I know one of those things is hitting home with you right about now. Spend some time thinking about how much you deserve to live in confidence. I can't think of anyone more deserving. You deserve to walk in confidence!

Reflection:

Take out a piece of paper or your journal and write down your answers to the following questions:

- Are you struggling with confidence in some area of your life? If so, list three of those areas.

- What are three practical ways you can overcome and combat your lack of confidence?

- How might owning your thoughts about yourself booster your confidence?

- How can mindful thinking apply to boosting your confidence?

Affirmation:

Stand before your mirror each day and say out loud:

I am beautiful in mind, body and soul. I embrace my flaws and walk confidently in who I am created to be.

Stay Determined

Get comfortable with being uncomfortable![35]

— Jillian Michaels

Have you ever met someone you admired and wondered how they were able to accomplish all the things they did? Or read about someone with a truly amazing and inspiring life story? I have, and her name is Dani Johnson, author and life coach. A few years ago, I was surfing the internet and ran across an interview in which she shared her story. It was one of triumph, resilience, and pure determination.

Dani was raised in a physically abusive household and was molested from the tender age of three until she turned sixteen. After years of abuse, she attempted suicide. Thank goodness that plan failed, or she wouldn't have been able to share her incredible and inspiring story with the world. As if the abuse and drug use wasn't enough, Dani also found herself living out of her car at one point. While living out of her car, she had an idea to start selling weight loss programs—the very same weight loss program she had purchased for herself months ago. Her initial thought was to sell the program as a means to pay for an apartment. In the beginning, she ran the business out of her car and a phone booth. That weight loss business went on to net her a quarter of a million dollars in the first year.[36]

How unbelievable is her story? I swear, every time I hear it, tears just roll down my face as I think about the years of pain she endured. But the important thing is: she bounced back. She had this determination inside of her to do better and she didn't give up when it would have been so easy to.

I shared Dani's story with you as an example of the power of determination, because no matter your path in life, you will need to develop resilience and determination. Determination is what will help you overcome difficult times in life or achieve your dreams, whether those dreams are to open a business or become the first person to graduate from college in your family.

Whatever it is you desire, it *can* be done, but you have to have unwavering faith and tenacity to achieve your dreams. So how do you develop that? These little tidbits can apply to any situation in life, so pay attention. The first thing you must do is figure out what you want to achieve. Do you want to become a mother, own your own business, attend medical school, or a get promotion at work? Think about your goal and always keep it in mind. This leads to my next point, which is to stay focused. It is easy to become distracted by people and circumstances. You will encounter naysayers along the way who would be comfortable if you stayed exactly where you are. This is what I call noise, and you have to get to the point where you feel confident enough to tune out the noise. I can promise you, the noise will come. Doubt, fear, and difficulty will come, but you have the power to decide whether to let those things deter you or to continue pushing forward. Which will you choose?

Reflection:

Take out a piece of paper or your journal. List three goals you would like to achieve. Below the list, answer these questions:

- Have you given up on a goal in the past? Why?

- How can you apply the principles learned in this chapter to your goals?

Look at your surroundings, take a deep breath, and imagine your new reality changing right in front of you. Then acknowledge that with just a little grit and determination, it can.

Greatness

***Before you find out who you are,
you have to figure out who you aren't.*** [37]
— Iyanla Vanzant

Close your eyes, take a deep breath, and imagine a powerful, grounded, unapologetic woman is standing in front of you. Now give yourself a round of applause, because that woman is YOU. That is who you will have to become to step into greatness. Greatness will require you to walk in your true power, to know your true worth, and to dissociate from people that don't recognize your value. It also means that sometimes, you will have to walk alone to discover who you are, your passions, and your beliefs. Stepping into greatness calls for you to be comfortable in your own skin; to speak your opinion unapologetically and to trust your gut.

It doesn't matter if you're twenty or eighty years old—you deserve to walk in your greatness. Don't let naysayers talk you out of your greatness because you are a certain age or because you come from a certain family background or ethnicity. Greatness knows no color, no boundaries, and no gender. It just recognizes greatness.

My beloveds, as our time together comes to an end I want to thank you for taking this ride with me. It has been my pleasure to serve as your guide. I hope you know how proud I am of you. I know it may not have been easy to reflect on your past and all the wounds this book may have opened.

Though we're at the end of this book, it is only the beginning of your new journey. Before we wrap up our time together, let me remind you that there is a strong powerful woman residing inside you. A queen ready to step into her greatness. She is so close; she's just waiting for you to meet her halfway. She is excited about her new life, and is waiting for you on the other side to acknowledge her and embrace her with open arms and a loving heart. Don't let her walk away. You are so close, you can literally feel her breath on your skin.

I know you and she haven't spent much time together; it may be a little scary at first. But I promise you, this is one relationship you don't want to walk away from. She understands your hesitation, and she will remain patient and loving as she waits for you to put aside your fear.

Imagine yourself unleashed. Powerful, relentless, and courageous. You, my sister, have everything you need inside of you. It will be an amazing journey as you step into greatness, and I am honored to have walked this path with you.

Reflection:

Last entry! Take out a piece of paper or your journal and write down your answers to the following questions:

- What areas in your life would you need to improve upon in order to step into your greatness?

- What will your life look like when you have fully accepted who you are and stepped into your greatness?

- What are you willing to do to unleash your greatness?

- What will you stop hiding in order to stand strong and step into your greatness?

- What relationships are you willing to let go of so that you can flourish?

- What relationships are you willing to grow so that you can flourish?

Just because our time together has come to a close doesn't mean that you can't continue on your journey of stepping into your greatness. Go back and re-read any chapters in the book as needed. I encourage you to continue to reflect on the tools in this book and apply them to your life. As you step into your greatness in the future, revisit the questions and answers you jotted down in your journal as a way to measure your progress.

As your journey unfolds I encourage you not to crawl, not to stride, but to step confidently and strongly into your greatness.

REFERENCES

1   Williamson, Marianne. A Return to Love: Reflections on the
    Principles of A Course in Miracles. HarperCollins

    Publishers, 1992.

2   @JoyceMeyer. "Just relax and let God be God." *Twitter*, 1 Jan. 2013, 8:00 p.m.,

    www.twitter.com/joycemeyer/status/286320915329994752. Accessed 8 Nov. 2017.

3   "Your Mental Attitude." *The James Allen Free Library*,

    james-allen.in1woord.nl/?text=above-lifes-turmoil#c10. Accessed 13 Dec. 2017.

4   "Frank Outlaw Quotes." *Beliefnet's Inspirational Quotes*, www.beliefnet.
    com/quotes/inspiration/f/frank-outlaw/watch-your-thoughts-they-
    become-words-watch-you.aspx. Accessed 10 Dec. 2017.

5   "Howard Thurman Center for Common Ground, Boston University." *Boston University*,

    www.bu.edu/thurman/about/history/. Accessed 8 Nov. 2017.

6   Hamlin, Rick. "10 Great C.S. Lewis Quotes on Prayer." *Guideposts*, 22 Nov. 2013,

    guideposts.org/faith-and-prayer/prayer-stories/pray-effectively/10-
    great-cs-lewis-quotes-on-prayer. Accessed 8 Nov. 2017.

7   Gaille, Brandon. "27 Cosmetics Industry Statistics and Trends."
    Brandon Gaille Marketing Expert & Blog Master,

    20 May 2017, www.brandongaille.com/26-cosmetics-industry-
    statistics-and-trends/. Accessed 8 Nov. 2017.

8   McBride Ph.D., Karyl. "Is Self-Care Selfish? How to take care
    of yourself and not feel guilty!" *Psychology Today*,

    10 Feb. 2013, www.psychologytoday.com/blog/the-legacy-distorted-
    love/201302/is-self-care-selfish. Accessed 10 Dec. 2017.

9   Galil, Leor. "Does Drake Own YOLO?" *Forbes*, 29 Dec. 2012, www.forbes.com/sites/leorgalil/2012/12/29/does-

drake-own-yolo/#591b7a212556. Accessed 15 Nov. 2017.

10   Mayo Clinic Staff. "Exercise: 7 Benefits of Regular Physical Activity." The Mayo Clinic, 13 Oct. 2016,

www.mayoclinic.org/healthy-lifestyle/fitness/in-depth/exercise/art-20048389/. Accessed 9 Nov. 2017.

11   "Stephanie Lahart Quotes." *Goodreads*, www.goodreads.com/author/quotes/7016687.Stephanie_Lahart.

Accessed 14 Sep. 2017.

12   Young Entrepreneur Council. "7 Ways Entrepreneurs Are Like Athletes." *Inc*, 27 Jan. 2016,

www.inc.com/young-entrepreneur-council/7-ways-entrepreneurs-are-like-athletes.html. Accessed 13 Nov. 2017.

13   Stewart B James. "In the Chamber of Secrets: J.K. Rowling's Net Worth." *New York Times*, 24 Nov. 2016,

www.forbes.com/profile/jk-rowling/. Accessed 13 Nov. 2017.

14   Jensen III, Lorenzo. "70 Inspirational Quotes About Letting Go and Moving On." *Thought Catalog*, 1 July 2015,

www.thoughtcatalog.com/lorenzo-jensen-iii/2015/07/70-inspirational-quotes-about-letting-go-and-moving-on/.

Accessed 13 Sep. 2017.

15   Robinson, Melia. "Tim Ferriss: 'You are the average of the five people you most associate with.'" *Business*

Insider, 11 Jan. 2017, www.businessinsider.com/tim-ferriss-average-of-five-people-2017-1. Accessed 15 Nov. 2017.

16 Schawbel, Dan. "Brene Brown: How Vulnerability Can Make Our Lives Better." *Forbes*, 21 Apr. 2013,

www.forbes.com/sites/danschawbel/2013/04/21/brene-brown-how-vulnerability-can-make-our-lives-

better/#507fa8ae36c7. Accessed 13 Nov. 2017.

17 "Stephen Richards Quotes." *Goodreads*, www.goodreads.com/quotes/tag/forgive-yourself.

Accessed 13 Sep. 2017.

18 Lowe, Lindsay. "100 Inspiring Quotes on Love and Marriage." *Parade*, 21 Apr. 2015,

www.parade.com/391231/lindsaylowe/100-inspiring-quotes-on-love-and-marriage/. Accessed 15 Nov. 2017.

19 "Oprah Winfrey Quotes." *BrainyQuote*,

www.brainyquote.com/quotes/quotes/o/oprahwinfr383372.html?src=t_instincts. Accessed 13 Sep. 2017.

20 Niecy Nash. "You Will Attract What You Are." *Essence*, 28 June 2013,

www.essence.com/2013/06/30/niecy-nash-you-will-attract-what-you-are. Accessed 13 Nov. 2017.

21 Haden, Jeff. "55 Motivational Quotes That Will Inspire You to Believe in Yourself." *Inc*, 5 Nov. 2015,

www.inc.com/jeff-haden/55-motivational-quotes-that-will-inspire-you-to-believe-in-yourself.html.

Accessed 13 Sep. 2017.

22 Statistic Brain. "Stress Statistics." *Statistic Brain*, 18 May 2017, www.statisticbrain.com/stress-statistics/.

Accessed 4 Nov. 2017.

23 Borchard, Therese. "25 Quotes that Will Help You Face Your Fears. Psych Central." *World of Psychology*, 7 Oct. 2017,

www.psychcentral.com/blog/archives/2017/10/07/25-quotes-that-will-help-you-face-your-fears/.

Accessed 13 Dec. 2017.

24 "fear." *Dictionary.com*, Houghton Mifflin Company, www.dictionary.com/browse/fear. Accessed 16 Nov. 2017.

25 Acosta, Gabriela. "Your Daily Reminder: 30 Quotes That Promote Self-Care." *University of Southern California*,

7 Apr. 2014, msw.usc.edu/mswusc-blog/your-daily-reminder-30-quotes-that-promote-self-care/.

Accessed 13 Sep. 2017.

26 "Benjamin Franklin Quotes." *BrainyQuote*,

www.brainyquote.com/quotes/quotes/b/benjaminfr387287.html?src=t_growth. Accessed 14 Sep. 2017.

27 "Thomas Szasz Quotes." *The Quote Garden*, www.quotegarden.com/self-discovery.html. Accessed 13 Nov. 2017.

28 Makedonas, Eleni. "The Journey of Self-Discovery! My Decision to Find Myself!" *HuffPost*, 9 Apr. 2015,

www.huffingtonpost.com/eleni-makedonas/the-journey-of-selfdsicvo_b_7028362.html. Accessed 28 Aug. 2017.

29 Buddha. "The Quote Archive." *tinybuddha*,

www.tinybuddha.com/wisdom-quotes/you-yourself-as-much-as-anybody-in-the-entire-universe-deserve-your-love-and-affection/. Accessed 13 Nov. 2017.

30 Acosta, Gabriela. "Your Daily Reminder: 30 Quotes That Promote Self-Care." *University of Southern California*,

7 Apr. 2014, msw.usc.edu/mswusc-blog/your-daily-reminder-30-quotes-that-promote-self-care/.

Accessed 13 Sep. 2017.

31 "Fred Rogers Quotes." *Goodreads,* www.goodreads.com/author/quotes/32106.Fred_Rogers. Accessed 6 Nov. 2017.

32 "George R.R. Martin Quotes." *Goodreads,* www.goodreads.com/quotes/408441-a-reader-lives-a-thousand-lives-before-he-dies-said. Accessed 11 Dec. 2017.

33 Haden, Jeff. "55 Motivational Quotes That Will Inspire You to Believe in Yourself." *Inc,* 5 Nov. 2015,

www.inc.com/jeff-haden/55-motivational-quotes-that-will-inspire-you-to-believe-in-yourself.html.

Accessed 13 Sep. 2017.

34 Windmill, Eric. "No One Can Make You Feel Inferior Without Your Consent." *Lifehack,*

www.lifehack.org/453162/no-one-can-make-you-feel-inferior-without-your-consent. Accessed 13 Nov. 2017.

35 "Jillian Michaels Quotes." *Goodreads,* www.goodreads.com/quotes/tag/determination. Accessed 16 Nov. 2017.

36 Ziegler, Maseena. "How One Woman Went from Homeless to Millionaire In Less Than Two Years." *Forbes,* 13

Feb. 2013, www.forbes.com/sites/crossingborders/2013/02/13/how-one-woman-went-from-homeless-to-millionaire-in-less-than-two-years/#41a45fabbb09. Accessed 16 Nov. 2017; Ziegler, Maseena. "One Woman's Triumph Over Homelessness: How Dani Johnson Beat The Odds And Made Millions." *Forbes,* 7 May 2013, www.forbes.com/sites/crossingborders/2013/05/07/how-one-woman-went-from-homeless-to-millionaire-in-less-than-two-years-part-2/#7be3abb6c3ad. Accessed 16 Nov. 2017.

37 "Iyanla Vanzant Quotes." *Goodreads,* www.goodreads.com/author/quotes/15508.Iyanla_Vanzant.

Accessed 14 Sep. 2017.

www.ingramcontent.com/pod-product-compliance
Lightning Source LLC
Chambersburg PA
CBHW071453070426
42452CB00039B/1310